I AM

A

t

Life With Allah

ABOUT UMMAH WELFARE TRUST

Recent decades have seen this final Ummah encounter unprecedented trials and calamities. Millions who have taken Allah ﷻ as their Lord and His final Messenger ﷺ as their guide have suffered and even perished amidst continuous wars, natural disasters and enforced poverty.

Ummah Welfare Trust, a UK-based Islamic charity that was founded in 2001, has strived to fulfil the rights of those in need by providing them assistance in areas of nutrition, education, health, shelter, income and spiritual well-being.

Alhamdulillah, donors' contributions have enabled the charity to help over 30 million of our brothers and sisters in the past two decades. May their Sadaqah increase their provisions, repel oncoming evils, and be a shade for them on the Day of Judgement.

Our Beloved Messenge ﷺ was indeed the greatest of people in giving charity. He never considered anything too much or too little to give. Attachment to this world was made insignificant to him and he called our Ummah to faith, virtue and success in the afterlife.

For this reason, Ummah Welfare Trust has increased its focus in recent years on da'wah and Islamic revivalism. Alhamdulillah, across the Ummah, the charity has increased support to Islamic schools, expanded the construction of masjids, and extended assistance to Islamic teachers and students.

By Allah's permission, the charity hopes that 'Life with Allah' will help to revive the hearts of the believers and, in turn, the condition of the Ummah. May Allah ﷻ strengthen it and accept it from us all.

☾100%☽

100% DONATIONS POLICY

Donations change and save lives. Every single penny that you donate is used solely for charitable efforts.

TRANSPARENT EXPENDITURE

Ummah Welfare Trust monitors every donation to ensure that Zakat, Sadaqah and Lillah funds are spent correctly.

MAKING A DIFFERENCE

Since 2001, Ummah Welfare Trust has delivered your donations to over 30 million people around the Ummah.

Life With Allah
Connecting to The Creator

ABOUT LIFE WITH ALLAH

Life With Allah is a da'wah initiative of Ummah Welfare Trust which aims to connect the creation to The Creator.

Our goal is to instil the love and ma'rifah (deep knowledge) of Allah ﷻ and His Messenger ﷺ in ourselves, our families and the wider Ummah.

We envision an Ummah that is connected to the Book of Allah; that savours the sweetness of worship and īmān; and that worships Allah with basīrah (sure knowledge and insight).

We hope to strengthen our īmān and nurture the īmān of our upcoming generations, enabling them to remain steadfast in this era of trials.

WHAT WE DO

- Produce and publish books and pamphlets (print and digital)
- Distribute banners and posters for masjids
- Share daily reminders via social media
- Develop educational resources
- Provide authentic Islamic content through our website and app

OUR AREAS OF FOCUS

Knowing
& Loving
Allah ﷻ

Knowing & Loving
The Messenger of
Allah ﷺ

The Journey
of the
Hereafter

The Heart:
Actions &
Diseases

Tasting the
Sweetness of
Salāh

The Qur'ān:
Your Best
Friend

Dhikr
& Du'ā'

Ramadān
& Fasting

Dhul Hijjah
& Hajj

CONTENTS

INTRODUCTION

All praise is for Allah ﷻ, the Lord of the worlds, who ordered us to supplicate to Him and who promised to answer. May peace and blessings be upon His beloved Messenger, Muḥammad ﷺ through whom we were guided and learnt to call on our Creator. And may peace and blessings be upon the Prophets, the Companions and those who follow their way.

In many āyāt (verses) of the Qur'ān, Allah ﷻ instructs the believers to call on Him. He praised His Messengers and Prophets who did so, saying, 'They were ever quick in doing good deeds, they used to call on Us in yearning and awe, and humble themselves before Us.' (21:90)

The act of du'ā', or calling on Allah ﷻ, is one of the most superior forms of worship in Islam. Allah ﷻ has commanded us to call on Him and humble ourselves to Him.

Sadly the value for du'ā' has diminished in our times. Our ignorance, neglect, and oftentimes laziness, in entreating Allah ﷻ with the choice words of the Qur'ān and Sunnah has resulted in us failing to garner the many bounties that Allah ﷻ has promised.

This small book is an attempt to revive the love of du'ā' through which we can achieve success. The first chapter of the book outlines the excellence and etiquettes of du'ā', as well as offering an explanation of the steps to follow during supplication.

This is followed by a chapter detailing praise (ḥamd) and salutations upon the Prophet ﷺ (ṣalawāt) that a reader can begin his du'ā' with. The next two chapters offer a comprehensive list of supplications from the Qur'ān and Sunnah, specifically ordered to cover the reader's every need.

For the sake of brevity, only the supplications from ṣaḥīḥ (authentic) and ḥasan (good) aḥadīth have been included in this publication. This does not mean that other supplications cannot be recited, as long as their meanings are sound.

In these days of trials and difficulties, fortunate is he who remains steadfast in calling upon his Lord. May Allah ﷻ make us from those who fear and beseech Him, and who are persistent and humble in doing so till our last breath.

Life With Allah
Muḥarram 1446 / July 2024

"When My servants ask you about Me,
truly I am near."

(2:186)

فضل الدعاء وآدابه

DU'Ā' AND
ITS METHOD

WHAT IS DU'Ā'?

Du'ā' is a whispering conversation with Allah 🙵, our Creator, Lord and Sustainer. We ask Him because only He can give. He has Power over everything, whilst we have none. His Knowledge encompasses everything, whilst we know little. He is the Lord and we are His slaves.

The Messenger of Allah 🙵 said: "There is nothing more honourable to Allah than du'ā'." He 🙵 also said: "Allah is angry with those who do not make du'ā' to Him." (Tirmidhī)

Asking Allah for our needs is an expression of our humility. It is through du'ā' that we affirm our helplessness and need for Allah 🙵. It is an expression of our complete submission and 'ubudiyyah (servitude) to Him. This is why the Messenger of Allah 🙵 said: "Du'ā' is worship." (Tirmidhī)

By making du'ā' we speak to Allah 🙵 directly. We do not need intermediaries or special permission, nor must we wait to access the court of Allah 🙵. We can ask Allah 🙵 instantly, anywhere, anytime. This intimacy and bond that we share is outlined in the āyah:

'When My servants ask you about Me, truly I am near. I answer the call of the caller when he calls on Me; so let them respond (with obedience) to Me, and believe in Me, so that they may be guided.' (2:186)

Duʿāʾ is truly a gift and should form an inseparable part of our lives.

'I do not worry about my duʿāʾ being answered. Rather, I worry about making duʿāʾ because I know that if I am inspired by Allah to make duʿāʾ, the answer will follow.'

'Umar ibn al-Khaṭṭāb ﷺ

Imām Aḥmad ﷺ was asked: 'What is the distance between us and the Throne of Allah?' He replied: 'A sincere duʿāʾ from a sincere heart'.

THE ETIQUETTE OF MAKING DU'Ā'

‹1› **Humble yourself** in front of Allah ﷻ, fearing His punishment and hoping for His reward. This is the essence and purpose of du'ā'. Allah ﷻ says: 'Supplicate to your Lord humbly and secretly... and supplicate to Him in fear and hope.' (7:55-6)

‹2› **Have yaqīn (firm conviction) that Allah ﷻ will answer your du'ā.** The Messenger of Allah ﷺ said: "Make du'ā to Allah ﷻ whilst you are certain of a response, because Allah ﷻ does not accept a du'ā from a heedless, distracted heart." (Tirmidhī)

‹3› **Be persistent.** The Messenger of Allah ﷺ said: "Verily your Lord is Generous and Shy. If His servant raises his hands to Him, He becomes shy to return them empty." (Tirmidhī)

Whoever keeps knocking on the door will eventually have it opened for him.

‹4› **Do not be impatient.** The Messenger of Allah ﷺ said: "The du'ā of every one of you is accepted as long as he does not grow impatient and says: 'I made du'ā but it was not accepted.'" (Muslim)

‹5› **Supplicate with du'ās from the Qur'ān and the Sunnah.** Although it is permissible to choose your own words according to your needs, the du'ās from the Qur'ān and Sunnah are unmatched in their style, prose and completeness.

‹6› **Avoid sinning and consuming ḥarām.** The Messenger of Allah ﷺ talked about a man beseeching Allah ﷻ, saying: 'O Lord! O Lord!' but "his food was unlawful, his drink was unlawful, his clothing was unlawful, and he was nourished with unlawful; so how will his du'ā' be accepted?!" (Muslim)

‹7› **Make abundant du'ā' in times of ease.** The Messenger of Allah ﷺ said: "Remember Allah during times of ease and He will remember you during times of hardship." (Aḥmad)

‹8› **Prepare properly.** Perform wuḍū, face the qiblah and raise your hands. These are not necessary for du'ā' but are praiseworthy nonetheless.

‹9› **Be ambitious and ask for everything.** Do not limit your supplications to just small matters in difficult times. Nothing is too big for the One being asked and nothing is too small for the one asking Him. The Messenger of Allah ﷺ said:

"When one of you asks for something from Allah, then let him be plentiful (in what he asks for), for indeed he is asking his Lord." (Ibn Ḥibbān)

In another ḥadīth, he told us: "When you ask Allah, ask for al-Firdaws (the highest level of Jannah)." (Tirmidhī)

⟨10⟩ **Do not become despondent.** Even after prolonged supplications and patience, you must not think that your duʿā' has been rejected. Remain optimistic and ignore the demoralising whispers of shayṭān. "Allah ﷻ says: 'I am just as My slave thinks I am and I am with him when he remembers Me.'" (Bukhārī)

The Messenger of Allah ﷺ said:

"No Muslim makes duʿā' which does not entail a sin or the severing of ties of kinship without Allah ﷻ giving him one of three:

⟨1⟩ He fulfils his duʿā' immediately.

⟨2⟩ He stores it for him in the hereafter.

⟨3⟩ He averts from him a similar evil."

The Companions ﷺ said: "If that is so, we will make duʿā' even more." He ﷺ replied: "Allah ﷻ will respond even more." (Aḥmad)

OCCASIONS WHEN DU'Ā' IS READILY ACCEPTED

Increase du'ā' in these times and situations

The end of the farḍ prayers
(Tirmidhī)

Between adhān and iqāmah
(Tirmidhī)

The last third part of the night
(Bukhārī)

Whilst in sajdah
(Muslim)

Whilst fasting and when opening the fast
(Tirmidhī)

The last portion of the day of Jumu'ah
(Abū Dāwūd)

Day of 'Arafah
(Tirmidhī)

When one asks Allah with His Greatest Name
(See page 18)

When drinking zamzam water
(Ibn Mājah)

When it rains
(Abū Dāwūd)

When travelling
(Tirmidhī)

For your absent brother
(Muslim)

When oppressed
(Bukhārī)

When a parent makes du'ā' for their child
(Tirmidhī)

FIVE STEPS TO FOLLOW IN DU'Ā'

STEP ONE
START WITH PRAISING ALLAH

The Messenger of Allah ﷺ said: "There is none who likes to be praised more than Allah does." (Bukhārī)

The Messenger of Allah ﷺ once heard a person making du'ā' during prayer. He did not glorify Allah ﷺ nor invoke ṣalawāt upon the Messenger of Allah ﷺ. The Messenger of Allah ﷺ said: 'He was too hasty.'

He called him and said: 'When one of you makes du'ā', he should start off with praising and glorifying His Lord ﷺ, and should then invoke ṣalawāt on the Prophet. He should then make du'ā' for whatever he wishes.' (Abū Dāwūd)

Praising Allah ﷺ is one of the most commendable acts a slave can perform. The Messenger of Allah ﷺ told us that the best words a slave can utter after the Qur'ān are the words of praise and glory. (Aḥmad) It is the only worship that will be performed by the inhabitants of Paradise; and will be the manner in which they ask from Allah ﷺ. Allah ﷺ says: 'Their call therein will be 'How Perfect You are, O Allah' and their greeting therein will be 'peace,' and the end of their call will be 'Praise be to Allah, Lord of the worlds.' (10:10)

The Messenger of Allah ﷺ also said: 'The inhabitants of Paradise... will praise and glorify Allah as easily as you breathe.' (Muslim)

When one reflects on the du'ās in the Qur'ān made by the Prophets, one marvels at the courtesy, shyness and humility which shine through their words. Each du'ā' is a testimony to their awareness of and deep intimacy with their Lord. Rather than rushing to make their requests, they praised Allah ﷻ, glorified Him, and asked through His Most Perfect Names.

We see this in the du'ās of the Messenger of Allah ﷺ. The ḥadīth of intercession mentions that the believers will ask various Prophets to intercede for them to Allah ﷻ. Upon their refusal, they will approach the Messenger of Allah ﷺ who will be given permission to present himself before Allah ﷻ. He ﷺ said:

"When I will see my Lord, I will fall down in prostration before Him and He will leave me in prostration as long as He wishes, and then it will be said to me: 'O Muḥammad! Raise your head and speak, for you will be listened to; and ask, for you will be granted your request; and intercede, for your intercession will be accepted.' I will then raise my head and praise my Lord with certain praises which He will inspire me, and then I will intercede." (Bukhārī)

Thus the Prophet's 🌸 special praise of His Lord will be a means for his intercession to be accepted.

The angels have also shown us how to make du'ā' by praising Allah 🐝. Before asking for forgiveness for 'those who have repented and followed Your way,' they initiated their du'ā' by saying: 'Our Lord, You have encompassed all things in mercy and knowledge…' (40:7)

Though many of us regularly make du'ā', we fail to use this gift of praising Allah 🐝. Sadly it does not spring from our hearts as it should because we have failed to recognise and know Allah 🐝 as He deserves to be known. Allah 🐝 says: 'They did not hold Allah in His true esteem.' (39:67) When we recognise the greatness, grandeur and glory of Allah 🐝, our praises for Him will flow easily and naturally.

How can we praise Allah 🐝?

⟨1⟩ We praise Him as He has praised Himself. This is the best way to praise Allah 🐝. This can be learnt by reciting the Qur'ān, reflecting upon it and forming a strong bond with it, since it is replete with Allah ﷻ praising Himself.

⟨2⟩ Praise Him as our beloved Messenger ﷺ praised Him. Of Allah's creation, none surpassed him in knowing Him and appreciating Him as He ought to be.

⟨3⟩ Praise Him with words used by the Companions ﷺ and the pious predecessors.

⟨4⟩ Praise Him with one's own words emanating from the heart, so long as it does not contradict sound beliefs.

⟨5⟩ One of the best ways of praising Allah ﷻ is through His Beautiful Names. (See page 15)

'The best slaves of Allah on the Day of Judgement will be those who frequently praise Him.'

(Tirmidhī)

STEP TWO
SEND ṢALAWĀT UPON THE MESSENGER OF ALLAH ﷺ

'Indeed, Allah and His angels send blessings to the Prophet. O you who believe, invoke Allah to bless him, and send your salām (prayer for his being in peace) to him in abundance.' (33:56)

What do the Ṣalawāt mean?

صَلِّ (صَلَّى / اَلصَّلَاةُ عَلَى النَّبِيِّ)

O Allah, have mercy upon Muḥammad and praise him in the lofty assembly i.e. amongst the elite angels who are close to Allah ﷻ.

Ṣalāh also means 'honour him' i.e. honour him in the world by elevating his mention, granting victory to his dīn and preserving his sharīʿah; and honour him in the hereafter by rewarding him abundantly, accepting his intercession on behalf of his ummah and granting him the loftiest station of glory (maqām maḥmūd). (Ibn Ḥajar quoting Ḥalīmī in Fatḥ al-Bārī)

سَلِّمْ (سَلَّمَ / اَلسَّلَامُ عَلَى النَّبِيِّ)

O Allah, send peace upon Muḥammad; protect him, keep him safe from harm and take care of him.

Thus ṣalāh is the acquisition of all good and salām is the protection from all evil. The Messenger of Allah ﷺ said: "The closest of people to me on the Day of Judgement will be those who send the most ṣalāh upon me." (Tirmidhī)

Why do we invoke Ṣalawāt upon the Messenger ﷺ?

Sending abundant ṣalāh upon the Messenger ﷺ is a manifestation of our love, reverence and obedience to him. He was sent as a mercy for mankind, and always remembered and worried about us.

On one occasion he ﷺ lifted his hands and while weeping, invoked: "O Allah! My ummah, my ummah!" Allah sent Jibrīl ﷺ down with the glad tidings: "Muḥammad, surely we will please you in regards to your ummah and we will not cause you grief." (Muslim)

In every ṣalāh, he ﷺ would ask Allah to forgive us. (Ibn Ḥibbān) He ﷺ missed us and yearned to see us. He ﷺ once said: "I wish to see my brothers!" The Companions ﷺ asked: "O Messenger of Allah, are we not your brothers?" He ﷺ replied: "You are my Companions, but my brothers are those who have not yet come in the world. I will welcome them at the ḥawḍ (blessed fountain)." (Nasā'ī)

Unlike the other Messengers who had their exclusive du'ā' accepted in this world, the Messenger ﷺ reserved his du'ā' for the Day of Judgement where he will intercede on our behalf. (Bukhārī)

'Du'ā' is suspended between the heaven and the earth and none of it ascends until you send salawāt upon your Prophet ﷺ.'

'Umar ibn al-Khaṭṭāb ﷺ

'Whoever wants to ask Allah for his needs, let him start by sending salawāt upon the Prophet ﷺ then ask for what he needs, and then end his du'ā' with salawāt (again) upon the Prophet ﷺ. For sending salawāt upon the Prophet ﷺ will be accepted, and Allah is too generous to refuse (the du'ā' made) between the two salawāt.'

Abū Sulaymān al-Dārānī ﷺ

STEP THREE

ASK ALLAH BY HIS BEAUTIFUL NAMES AND HIS ONENESS

Allah ﷻ says in the Noble Qurʾān:

وَلِلَّهِ الْأَسْمَاءُ الْحُسْنَىٰ فَادْعُوهُ بِهَا.

'To Allah belong the Most Beautiful Names, so call on Him by them.' (7:180)

Calling on Allah ﷻ means praising and worshipping Him with His Beautiful Names, and making duʿāʾ to Him with them.

An example of this is in the ḥadīth of Buraydah ؓ who narrated that the Messenger of Allah ﷺ heard a man saying:

اَللّٰهُمَّ إِنِّي أَسْأَلُكَ بِأَنِّي أَشْهَدُ بِأَنَّكَ أَنْتَ اللهُ لَا إِلٰهَ إِلَّا أَنْتَ الْأَحَدُ الصَّمَدُ الَّذِي لَمْ يَلِدْ وَلَمْ يُولَدْ وَلَمْ يَكُنْ لَّهُ كُفُوًا أَحَدٌ.

"O Allah, I ask You as I bear witness that You are Allah, there is no-one worthy of worship but You, the One, the Self-Sufficient Master, who has not given birth and was not born, and to whom no one is equal."

The Messenger of Allah ﷺ remarked: "By the One in whose Hand is my life, he has certainly asked Allah with His Greatest Name; when He is supplicated by it, He responds, and when asked, He gives." (Tirmidhī)

He ﷺ also said: "Supplicate frequently with:

$$\text{يَا ذَا الْجَلَالِ وَالْإِكْرَامِ}$$

(O Lord of Majesty and Honour)." (Tirmidhī)

Calling upon Allah through His Oneness is one of the most powerful ways to make duʿā. The grief-stricken Prophet Yunus ﷺ cried out to his Lord:

$$\text{لَا إِلَهَ إِلَّا أَنْتَ سُبْحَانَكَ إِنِّي كُنْتُ مِنَ الظَّالِمِينَ.}$$

The Prophet ﷺ said that no one supplicates with this duʿā except that his supplication is accepted. And nobody supplicates with it except that Allah ﷻ removes his difficulties. (Tirmidhī) (See page 56)

In this duʿā, Yunus ﷺ asked Allah ﷻ through the following steps (known as tawassul in Arabic):

⟨1⟩ Invoking the Oneness of Allah ﷻ and affirming that no one deserves to be worshipped except Him.

⟨2⟩ Declaring Allah's absolute perfection and negating any faults from Him.

⟨3⟩ Acknowledging one's own wrongdoing.

The Messenger of Allah ﷺ said: "Indeed Allah has 99 Names; whoever preserves them will enter Paradise." (Muslim)

Preserving them includes:

⟨1⟩ Memorising them.

⟨2⟩ Understanding their meanings.

⟨3⟩ Praising Allah ﷻ and calling upon Him through them.

⟨4⟩ Acting upon what they necessitate.

How Can I Ask with Allah's Names?

Ask Allah ﷻ with His Greatest Names. Relevant Names can also be called upon for specific requests. For example, 'Yā Tawwāb (O Acceptor of repentance), accept my repentance.' Remove the 'al' when invoking Allah with His Names; so you would say 'Yā Razzāq' and not 'Yā al-Razzāq,' for example.

> 'Whoever attains the ma'rifah (deep awareness) of Allah through His Names, Attributes and Actions, will undoubtedly love Him.'
>
> Ibn al-Qayyim ﷺ

أَسْمَاءُ الله الْحُسْنَى

THE GREATEST NAMES OF ALLAH
with which, when invoked, He responds

اَلرَّحْمٰنُ

The
All-Merciful

اَلرَّبُّ

The
Lord

اَلْأَوَّلُ

The
First

اَلصَّمَدُ

The
Self-Sufficient
Master

اَلْأَحَدُ

The
Single

اَلرَّحِيمُ

The
Very Merciful

اَلْحَيُّ

The
Ever-Living

اَلْبَاطِنُ

The
Most Close

اَلظَّاهِرُ

The
Most High

اَلْآخِرُ

The
Last

ذُوالْجَلَالِ وَالْإِكْرَامِ

The
Lord of Majesty and Honour

اَلْمَنَّانُ

The
Bestower

اَلْقَيُّومُ

The
All-Sustainer

Names which lead to
**THE FEAR
OF ALLAH**
and constant awareness
of Him

The
Witness

The
Vigilant

The
All-Aware

The
All-Knowing

The
Ever-Watchful

The
All-Seeing

The
All-Hearing

19

The
Giver

Names which inspire
PATIENCE AND GRATITUDE

The
Most Generous

The
All-Comprehending

The
Ever-Giving

The
Supreme Provider

The
Supreme Opener

The
Curer

The
Most Appreciative

The
Grateful

The
Doer of Good

The
All-Wise

The
Independent

The
Light

The
Guide

Names which inspire
TRUST IN ALLAH

The
Protector

The
Helper

The
**Protective
Friend**

The
Master

The
All-Sufficient

The
**Powerful /
Nourisher**

The
**Sufficient /
Reckoner**

The
Guardian

The
Responder

The
Ever-Near

The
**Disposer
of Affairs**

The
Guarantor

Names which inspire
THE GREATNESS OF ALLAH
and prompt us to exalt Him

The
Mighty

The
Sovereign

The
King

The
Owner

The
Powerful

The
All-Dominant

The
Irresistible

The
Compellor / Restorer

The
Invincible

The
Strong

The
All-Able

The
All-Powerful

The
One

The
Supremely Proud

The
Most Great

The
Magnificent

The
Exalted

The
Highest

The
High

The
**One Who
has no Equal**

The
Judge

The
**Supremely
Glorified**

The
**Source of
Peace**

The
Pure

The
Evident

The
Truth

The
**Supreme
Judge**

The
Just

The
**Giver of
Security**

The
**All-
Encompassing**

The
**Most
Glorious**

The
Inheritor

The
**Most
Forgiving**

Names which inspire us to
LOVE ALLAH
and show due
respect to Him

The
Forgiving

The
**Most Kind/
Subtle**

The
**Acceptor of
Repentance**

The
**Most
Compassionate**

The
**Ever-
Pardoning**

The
**Concealer
of Sins**

The
Modest

The
Kind

The
Forbearing

The
Creator

The
Originator

The
**Most
Bountiful**

The
Generous

الرَّفِيْقُ

The
Most Gentle

الْمُصَوِّرُ

The
Fashioner

الْبَارِئُ

The
Inventor

الْخَلَّاقُ

The
Supreme Creator

الْوَدُوْدُ

The
Most Loving

الطَّيِّبُ

The
Pure

الْجَمِيْلُ

The
Beautiful

الْحَمِيْدُ

The
Praised

وَلِلَّهِ الْأَسْمَاءُ الْحُسْنَى

"To Allah belongs the Most Beautiful
Names, so call on Him by them."

(7:180)

SEEK FORGIVENESS

Before you ask Allah ﷻ for anything, you should always ask Him to forgive you. He is al-Ghafūr (The Most Forgiving) and loves to forgive. He ﷻ reminds us in the Noble Qur'ān:

'Say: 'My slaves, those who have transgressed against themselves, do not despair of the mercy of Allah. Truly Allah forgives all sins: He is truly the Most Forgiving, the Most Merciful." (39:53)

The Messenger of Allah ﷺ said: "Allah, Exalted is He, said: 'Son of Ādam, as long as you call upon me and hope in Me, I will forgive you irrespective of what you do, and I do not care. Son of Ādam, even if your sins were to reach to the clouds of the sky, then you seek forgiveness from Me, I will forgive you. Son of Ādam, even if you were to come to Me with nearly an earth full of sins, and then you meet me, not having associated anything with me, then I will surely bring you as much as the earth in forgiveness."' (Tirmidhī)

From this ḥadīth, Ibn Rajab ﷺ outlined three means of attaining forgiveness:

⟨1⟩ Calling upon Allah ﷻ with hope, knowing that only He forgives.

‹2› Asking Allah ﷻ for forgiveness, despite the magnitude of one's sins.

‹3› Actualising tawḥīd (the oneness of Allah ﷻ). This is the greatest means of forgiveness. If even a speck of tawḥīd was placed on a mountain of sins, it would turn the sins into good deeds.

An excellent du'ā' which combines all of the above is Sayyid al-Istighfār. (See the first du'ā' on page 75)

When seeking forgiveness, try to feel remorse in your heart, cry over your sins and beg Allah to forgive you. Ibn Rajab ﷺ said: 'People! Your hearts are essentially pure, but they have been stained with splashes of sins. So splash on them in turn the tears of your eyes and you will find your hearts purified.'

It is also virtuous to seek forgiveness for all of the believers. The Prophet ﷺ told us: "Whoever seeks forgiveness for every male and female believer, Allah will record a good deed for him for every male and female believer." (Ṭabarānī)

STEP FIVE
ENACT THE SECRET OF DU'Ā'

The secret to making du'ā' is to display one's dire need of Allah ﷻ, with utmost humility and desperation.

Our beloved Messenger ﷺ was the perfect embodiment of servitude. After years of struggle conveying the message of His Lord, the whole of the Arabian Peninsula comes under his control and finally accepts his message. Yet gathered on the plains of 'Arafah, as their leader, we do not witness parades or displays of pomp. Instead, we see the words of a true slave. He raises his blessed hands to Allah ﷻ and says:

"O Allah, You hear my speech… I am the desperate and needy one, the one who is seeking Your help and protection, fearful and scared, the one who confesses and acknowledge his sins. I beg You - **the begging of a destitute**; I humbly implore You - the imploring of a humiliated sinner. I invoke You - the invoking of the fearful afflicted person, whose neck is bowed down before You, whose eyes have overflowed with tears for You, whose body is humbled before You, and who has completely abased Himself to You…" (Ṭabarānī)

At his highest point of victory, we witness nothing but humility and turning to Allah ﷻ in desperate need.

Another example is from the great Prophet Musa 🕊,
whilst he is fleeing one of history's greatest tyrants.
He is forced into exile to Madyan where he is left
penniless, scared, hungry and alone; a foreigner in a
strange land. Instead of wallowing in self-pity, we see
his chivalry as he helps two young women to water
their animals. He then withdraws into the shade and
turns to the One Free of all need and begs: "My Lord,
I am **in dire need** of whatever good thing You may
send me." (28:24)

Breaking down in utter desperation and begging
Allah 🕊 is how we should make du'ā' on a daily basis,
as though our lives depended on it and we could not
survive without it. The person who is in his home
living comfortably is no less in need of his Lord than
the person who is clinging on to a piece of wood in
the middle of the ocean trying to save himself from
drowning. The Almighty 🕊 reminds us: 'People! It is
you who stand in need of God, whereas He Alone is
Free of all needs, Worthy of all praise.' (35:15)

We are weak and in need of Allah 🕊 for everything.
We cannot do without Him for the blink of an eye. So
let us beg Allah 🕊 whole-heartedly and sincerely and
we will witness the gifts from al-Wahhāb (The Ever-
Giving) shower into our lives.

THE OPTIMAL GUIDE FOR MAKING DU'Ā'

1 Make your heart present and completely focus on Allah ☉.

2 Choose a time in which du'ā' is readily accepted.

3 Perform wuḍū, face the qiblah and raise your hands.

4 Humble yourself and submit to Allah ☉.

5 Start by praising Allah ☉.

6 Send ṣalawāt upon the Prophet ﷺ.

7 Repent for your sins and ask for forgiveness.

8 Ask with persistence, love and fear.

9 Ask Allah through His Oneness and Names.

10 Give ṣadaqah before making du'ā'.

(Adapted from Ibn al-Qayyim's ☉ al-Jawāb al-Kāfī)

الحمد والثناء على الله

والصلاة على النبي

PRAISES OF ALLAH ﷻ
AND SALUTATIONS
UPON THE MESSENGER
OF ALLAH ﷺ

‹1› All praise is for Allah who has not taken a son, has no partner in His dominion and does not need anyone, out of weakness, to protect Him... (17:111)

‹2› All praise is for Allah who created the heavens and the earth and made darkness and light... (6:1)

‹3› All praise is for Allah who sent down the Book to His servant and did not place in it any crookedness. (18:1)

‹4› All praise is for Allah, to whom belongs all that is in the heavens and all that is on the earth; and for Him is all praise in the Hereafter. He is the All-Wise, the All-Aware. (34:1)

‹5› All praise is for Allah, the Originator of the heavens and the earth, who appoints the angels as messengers having wings, in twos, threes and fours. He adds to the creation what He wills. Indeed, Allah is All-Powerful over every thing. (35:1)

‹۱› اَلْحَمْدُ لِلّٰهِ الَّذِي لَمْ يَتَّخِذْ وَلَدًا وَّلَمْ يَكُنْ لَّهُ شَرِيكٌ فِي الْمُلْكِ وَلَمْ يَكُنْ لَّهُ وَلِيٌّ مِّنَ الذُّلِّ...

‹۲› اَلْحَمْدُ لِلّٰهِ الَّذِي خَلَقَ السَّمٰوٰتِ وَالْأَرْضَ وَجَعَلَ الظُّلُمٰتِ وَالنُّوْرَ...

‹۳› اَلْحَمْدُ لِلّٰهِ الَّذِي أَنْزَلَ عَلَىٰ عَبْدِهِ الْكِتٰبَ وَلَمْ يَجْعَلْ لَّهُ عِوَجًا.

‹۴› اَلْحَمْدُ لِلّٰهِ الَّذِي لَهُ مَا فِي السَّمٰوٰتِ وَمَا فِي الْأَرْضِ وَلَهُ الْحَمْدُ فِي الْأٰخِرَةِ وَهُوَ الْحَكِيمُ الْخَبِيرُ.

‹۵› اَلْحَمْدُ لِلّٰهِ فَاطِرِ السَّمٰوٰتِ وَالْأَرْضِ جَاعِلِ الْمَلٰئِكَةِ رُسُلًا أُولِي أَجْنِحَةٍ مَّثْنَىٰ وَثُلٰثَ وَرُبٰعَ، يَزِيدُ فِي الْخَلْقِ مَا يَشَاءُ، إِنَّ اللهَ عَلَىٰ كُلِّ شَيْءٍ قَدِيرٌ.

‹6› O Allah, for You Alone is all praise; You are the Light of the heavens and the earth and whatever is therein. For You Alone is all praise; You are the Maintainer of the heavens and the earth and whatever is therein. And for You Alone is all praise; You are the Truth. Your promise is the truth, Your Speech is the truth, the meeting with You is the truth, Paradise is the truth, Hell-Fire is the truth, the Final Hour is the truth, the Prophets are the truth and Muḥammad ﷺ is the truth. O Allah, I surrender myself to You Alone, I put my trust in You Alone, I believe in You Alone, I turn to You Alone, I complain of my opponents to You Alone and I refer judgement to You Alone. (Bukhārī)

‹7› O Allah, for You Alone is all praise. O Allah, none can restrict what You expand and none can expand what You have restricted. None can guide whom You have left astray, and none can mislead whom You have guided. None can give what You withhold, and none can withhold what You bestow. None can bring near what You have distanced and none can distance what You have brought near. (Aḥmad)

‹٦› اَللّٰهُمَّ لَكَ الْحَمْدُ، أَنْتَ نُورُ السَّمٰوٰاتِ وَالْأَرْضِ وَمَنْ فِيهِنَّ، وَلَكَ الْحَمْدُ أَنْتَ قَيِّمُ السَّمٰوٰاتِ وَالْأَرْضِ وَمَنْ فِيهِنَّ، وَلَكَ الْحَمْدُ، أَنْتَ الْحَقُّ وَوَعْدُكَ حَقٌّ، وَقَوْلُكَ حَقٌّ، وَلِقَاؤُكَ حَقٌّ، وَالْجَنَّةُ حَقٌّ، وَالنَّارُ حَقٌّ، وَالسَّاعَةُ حَقٌّ، وَالنَّبِيُّونَ حَقٌّ، وَمُحَمَّدٌ حَقٌّ، اللَّهُمَّ لَكَ أَسْلَمْتُ وَعَلَيْكَ تَوَكَّلْتُ وَبِكَ آمَنْتُ، وَإِلَيْكَ أَنَبْتُ، وَبِكَ خَاصَمْتُ، وَإِلَيْكَ حَاكَمْتُ.

‹٧› اَللّٰهُمَّ لَكَ الْحَمْدُ كُلُّهُ، اَللّٰهُمَّ لَا قَابِضَ لِمَا بَسَطْتَ، وَلَا بَاسِطَ لِمَا قَبَضْتَ، وَلَا هَادِيَ لِمَنْ أَضْلَلْتَ، وَلَا مُضِلَّ لِمَنْ هَدَيْتَ، وَلَا مُعْطِيَ لِمَا مَنَعْتَ، وَلَا مَانِعَ لِمَا أَعْطَيْتَ، وَلَا مُقَرِّبَ لِمَا بَاعَدْتَ، وَلَا مُبَاعِدَ لِمَا قَرَّبْتَ.

‹8› O Allah, Lord of the heavens and the earth, Lord of the Magnificent Throne, our Lord and Lord of all things, Splitter of the seed and the date stone, the One who revealed the Torah, the Bible and the Criterion (Qur'ān); I seek Your protection from the evil of every thing You hold by the forehead (i.e. fully control). You are the First and there is nothing before You. You are the Last and there is nothing after You. You are the Most High and there is nothing above You. You are the Most Near and there is nothing closer than You. (Muslim)

‹9› O Allah, Our Lord, to You Alone belongs all praise; praise which fills the heavens and the earth and which fills whatever You wish after that. You are Most worthy of praise and glory. The greatest truth the slave can utter is - and we are all Your slaves - there is none who can withhold what You give, and none can give what You withhold; and the wealth of the wealthy does not avail him from You. (Abū Dāwūd)

«٨» اَللّٰهُمَّ رَبَّ السَّمٰوَاتِ وَرَبَّ الْأَرْضِ وَرَبَّ الْعَرْشِ الْعَظِيمِ ، رَبَّنَا وَرَبَّ كُلِّ شَيْءٍ ، فَالِقَ الْحَبِّ وَالنَّوٰى ، وَمُنْزِلَ التَّوْرَاةِ وَالْإِنْجِيلِ وَالْفُرْقَانِ ، أَعُوذُ بِكَ مِنْ شَرِّ كُلِّ شَيْءٍ أَنْتَ آخِذٌ بِنَاصِيَتِهِ، اَللّٰهُمَّ أَنْتَ الْأَوَّلُ فَلَيْسَ قَبْلَكَ شَيْءٌ ، وَأَنْتَ الْآخِرُ فَلَيْسَ بَعْدَكَ شَيْءٌ ، وَأَنْتَ الظَّاهِرُ فَلَيْسَ فَوْقَكَ شَيْءٌ ، وَأَنْتَ الْبَاطِنُ فَلَيْسَ دُونَكَ شَيْءٌ.

«٩» اَللّٰهُمَّ رَبَّنَا لَكَ الْحَمْدُ مِلْءَ السَّمٰوَاتِ وَمِلْءَ الْأَرْضِ وَمِلْءَ مَا شِئْتَ مِنْ شَيْءٍ بَعْدُ ، أَهْلَ الثَّنَاءِ وَالْمَجْدِ ، أَحَقُّ مَا قَالَ الْعَبْدُ - وَكُلُّنَا لَكَ عَبْدٌ - لَا مَانِعَ لِمَا أَعْطَيْتَ ، وَلَا مُعْطِيَ لِمَا مَنَعْتَ ، وَلَا يَنْفَعُ ذَا الْجَدِّ مِنْكَ الْجَدُّ.

‹10› All praise is for Allah, Lord of the worlds, the All-Merciful, the Very Merciful, Master of the Day of Judgement. There is no god worthy of worship except You, You do what You will. O Allah, You are Allah, there is no god worthy of worship except You. You are the Rich and Free of all needs whilst we are poor and in need of You. (Ibn Ḥibbān)

‹11› All praise is for Allah who has sufficed me and given me refuge. All praise is for Allah who has fed me and given me drink. All praise is for Allah who has been gracious to me and showered favours on me. O Allah, I ask You by Your glory to save me from the Hell-fire. (Ḥākim)

‹12› All praise is for Allah who feeds and is not fed. He favoured us, and thus guided us, blessed us with food and drink, and bestowed upon us every favour. All praise is for Allah, a praise which we will never bid farewell to, a never-ending praise, an accepted praise and an indispensable praise. All praise is for Allah who provided food and drink; who clothed us, guided us from error, removed our blindness and favoured us greatly over many of His creation. All praise is for Allah, Lord of the worlds. (Nasā'ī)

«١٠» اَلْحَمْدُ لِلَّهِ رَبِّ الْعَالَمِينَ ، الرَّحْمٰنِ الرَّحِيمِ ، مَالِكِ يَوْمِ الدِّينِ، لَا إِلٰهَ إِلَّا أَنْتَ تَفْعَلُ مَا تُرِيدُ، اَللّٰهُمَّ أَنْتَ اللهُ لَا إِلٰهَ إِلَّا أَنْتَ ، أَنْتَ الْغَنِيُّ وَنَحْنُ الْفُقَرَاءُ.

«١١» اَلْحَمْدُ لِلَّهِ الَّذِي كَفَانِي وَآوَانِي ، اَلْحَمْدُ لِلَّهِ الَّذِي أَطْعَمَنِي وَسَقَانِي، اَلْحَمْدُ لِلَّهِ الَّذِي مَنَّ عَلَيَّ فَأَفْضَلَ، اَللّٰهُمَّ إِنِّي أَسْأَلُكَ بِعِزَّتِكَ أَنْ تُنَجِّيَنِي مِنَ النَّارِ.

«١٢» اَلْحَمْدُ لِلَّهِ الَّذِي يُطْعِمُ وَلَا يُطْعَمُ ، مَنَّ عَلَيْنَا فَهَدَانَا وَأَطْعَمَنَا وَسَقَانَا، وَكُلَّ بَلَاءٍ حَسَنٍ أَبْلَانَا، اَلْحَمْدُ لِلَّهِ غَيْرَ مُوَدَّعٍ وَلَا مُكَافَأٍ وَلَا مَكْفُورٍ وَلَا مُسْتَغْنًى عَنْهُ، اَلْحَمْدُ لِلَّهِ الَّذِي أَطْعَمَ مِنَ الطَّعَامِ، وَسَقَى مِنَ الشَّرَابِ ، وَكَسَا مِنَ الْعُرْيِ ، وَهَدَى مِنَ الضَّلَالَةِ، وَبَصَّرَ مِنَ الْعَمَى، وَفَضَّلَ عَلَى كَثِيرٍ مِّنْ خَلْقِهِ تَفْضِيلًا، اَلْحَمْدُ لِلَّهِ رَبِّ الْعَالَمِينَ.

‹13› All praise is for Allah; praise which is abundant, pure, blessed and perpetual, as our Lord loves and is pleased with. (Nasāʾī)

‹14› Glory be to Allah as much as all He has created. Glory be to Allah as much as what can fill His creation. Glory be to Allah as much as what is in the earth and the sky. Glory be to Allah as much as what can fill the earth and the sky. Glory be to Allah as much as as what His Book has recorded. Glory be to Allah as much as what fills His Book. Glory be to Allah as much as everything. Glory be to Allah as much as what fills everything. All praise is for Allah as much as what He has created. All praise is for Allah as much as what can fill His creation. All praise is for Allah as much as what is in the earth and the sky. All praise is for Allah as much as what can fill up the earth and the sky. All praise is for Allah as much as what His Book has recorded. All praise is for Allah as much as what fills His Book. All praise is for Allah as much as everything. All praise is for Allah as much as what fills everything. (Composite: Aḥmad & Ibn Ḥibbān)

‏(١٣) اَلْحَمْدُ لِلهِ حَمْدًا كَثِيرًا طَيِّبًا مُبَارَكًا فِيهِ مُبَارَكًا عَلَيْهِ ، كَمَا يُحِبُّ رَبُّنَا وَيَرْضَى.

‏(١٤) سُبْحَانَ اللهِ عَدَدَ مَا خَلَقَ ، وَسُبْحَانَ اللهِ مِلْءَ مَا خَلَقَ ، وَسُبْحَانَ اللهِ عَدَدَ مَا فِي الْأَرْضِ وَالسَّمَاءِ ، وَسُبْحَانَ اللهِ مِلْءَ مَا فِي الْأَرْضِ وَالسَّمَاءِ ، وَسُبْحَانَ اللهِ عَدَدَ مَا أَحْصَى كِتَابُهُ ، وَسُبْحَانَ اللهِ مِلْءَ مَا أَحْصَى كِتَابُهُ ، وَسُبْحَانَ اللهِ عَدَدَ كُلِّ شَيْءٍ ، وَسُبْحَانَ اللهِ مِلْءَ كُلِّ شَيْءٍ ، اَلْحَمْدُ لِلهِ عَدَدَ مَا خَلَقَ ، وَالْحَمْدُ لِلهِ مِلْءَ مَا خَلَقَ ، وَالْحَمْدُ لِلهِ عَدَدَ مَا فِي الْأَرْضِ وَالسَّمَاءِ ، وَالْحَمْدُ لِلهِ مِلْءَ مَا فِي الْأَرْضِ وَالسَّمَاءِ ، وَالْحَمْدُ لِلهِ عَدَدَ مَا أَحْصَى كِتَابُهُ ، وَالْحَمْدُ لِلهِ مِلْءَ مَا أَحْصَى كِتَابُهُ ، وَالْحَمْدُ لِلهِ عَدَدَ كُلِّ شَيْءٍ ، وَالْحَمْدُ لِلهِ مِلْءَ كُلِّ شَيْءٍ.

‹15› How perfect are You O Allah, and all praise is Yours. Your name is most blessed, Your majesty is exalted and there is no god worthy of worship except You. (Muslim)

‹16› Allah is free from imperfection and all praise is for Him. Allah, the Magnificent, is free from imperfection. (Bukhārī)

‹17› Allah is free from imperfection and all praise is for Him, (in ways) as numerous as all He has created, (as vast) as His pleasure, (as limitless) as the weight of His Throne, and (as endless) as the ink of His words. (Muslim)

‹18› How free from imperfection is the Owner of might, dominion, magnificence and greatness. (Nasāʾī)

‹19› The Supremely Perfect, the Most Pure, the Lord of the angels and the Spirit (Jibrīl). (Muslim)

﴾١٥﴿ سُبْحَانَكَ اللّٰهُمَّ وِبِحَمْدِكَ ، وَتَبَارَكَ اسْمُكَ ، وَتَعَالَى جَدُّكَ وَلَا إِلٰهَ غَيْرُكَ.

﴾١٦﴿ سُبْحَانَ اللهِ وَبِحَمْدِهِ ، سُبْحَانَ اللهِ الْعَظِيمِ.

﴾١٧﴿ سُبْحَانَ اللهِ وَبِحَمْدِهِ ، عَدَدَ خَلْقِهِ ، وَرِضَا نَفْسِهِ ، وَزِنَةَ عَرْشِهِ ، وَمِدَادَ كَلِمَاتِهِ.

﴾١٨﴿ سُبْحَانَ ذِي الْجَبَرُوتِ ، وَالْمَلَكُوتِ ، وَالْكِبْرِيَاءِ ، وَالْعَظَمَةِ.

﴾١٩﴿ سُبُّوحٌ ، قُدُّوسٌ ، رَبُّ الْمَلَائِكَةِ وَالرُّوحِ.

‹20› Allah is truly the Greatest. Praise be to Allah in abundance. Glory be to Allah in the morning and the evening. (Muslim)

‹21› There is no god worthy of worship except Allah, the One, the Supremely Powerful; Lord of the heavens and the earth and whatever is in between them, the All-Mighty, the Most Forgiving. (Ibn Ḥibbān)

‹22› There is no god worthy of worship except Allah. He is Alone and He has no partner whatsoever. To Him Alone belong all sovereignty and all praise. He is over all things All-Powerful. Allah is free from imperfection, and all praise is for Allah. There is no god worthy of worship except Allah and Allah is the Greatest. There is no power (in averting evil) or strength (in attaining good) except through Allah, the Most High, the Most Magnificent. (Ibn Mājah)

«۲۰» اَللهُ أَكْبَرُ كَبِيرًا ، وَالْحَمْدُ لِلهِ كَثِيرًا ، وَسُبْحَانَ اللهِ بُكْرَةً وَأَصِيلًا.

«۲۱» لَا إِلَهَ إِلَّا اللهُ الْوَاحِدُ الْقَهَّارُ ، رَبُّ السَّمَوَاتِ وَالْأَرْضِ وَمَا بَيْنَهُمَا الْعَزِيزُ الْغَفَّارُ.

«۲۲» لَا إِلَهَ إِلَّا اللهُ وَحْدَهُ لَا شَرِيكَ لَهُ ، لَهُ الْمُلْكُ وَلَهُ الْحَمْدُ ، وَهُوَ عَلَى كُلِّ شَيْءٍ قَدِيرٌ ، سُبْحَانَ اللهِ وَالْحَمْدُ لِلهِ وَلَا إِلَهَ إِلَّا اللهُ وَاللهُ أَكْبَرُ ، وَلَا حَوْلَ وَلَا قُوَّةَ إِلَّا بِاللهِ الْعَلِيِّ الْعَظِيمِ.

❮23❯ There is no god worthy of worship except Allah, the Magnificent, The Forbearing. There is no god worthy of worship except Allah, Lord of the Magnificent Throne. There is no god worthy of worship except Allah, Lord of the heavens, Lord of the earth and Lord of the Noble Throne. (Bukhārī)

❮24❯ There is no god worthy of worship except Allah, the Forbearing, the Most Generous. There is no god worthy of worship except Allah, the Most High, the Magnificent. Allah is free from imperfection, Lord of the seven heavens and the Lord of the Magnificent Throne. All praise is for Allah, Lord of the worlds. (Aḥmad)

❮25❯ O Allah, I call upon You, Your angels, the bearers of Your Throne, and all those in the heavens and the earth to bear witness that surely You are Allah. There is no god but You Alone. You have no partner whatsoever, and I bear witness that Muḥammad ﷺ is Your slave and Your Messenger. (Ḥākim)

﴿٢٣﴾ لَا إِلٰهَ إِلَّا اللهُ الْعَظِيْمُ الْحَلِيْمُ، لَا إِلٰهَ إِلَّا اللهُ رَبُّ الْعَرْشِ الْعَظِيْمِ، لَا إِلٰهَ إِلَّا اللهُ رَبُّ السَّمٰوَاتِ وَرَبُّ الْأَرْضِ وَرَبُّ الْعَرْشِ الْكَرِيْمِ.

﴿٢٤﴾ لَا إِلٰهَ إِلَّا اللهُ الْحَلِيْمُ الْكَرِيْمُ، لَا إِلٰهَ إِلَّا اللهُ الْعَلِيُّ الْعَظِيْمُ، سُبْحَانَ اللهِ رَبِّ السَّمٰوَاتِ السَّبْعِ وَرَبِّ الْعَرْشِ الْعَظِيْمِ، اَلْحَمْدُ لِلهِ رَبِّ الْعَالَمِيْنَ.

﴿٢٥﴾ اَللّٰهُمَّ إِنِّيْ أُشْهِدُكَ، وَأُشْهِدُ مَلَائِكَتَكَ وَحَمَلَةَ عَرْشِكَ، وَأُشْهِدُ مَنْ فِي السَّمٰوَاتِ وَمَنْ فِي الْأَرْضِ أَنَّكَ أَنْتَ اللهُ لَا إِلٰهَ إِلَّا أَنْتَ وَحْدَكَ، لَا شَرِيْكَ لَكَ، وَأَشْهَدُ أَنَّ مُحَمَّدًا عَبْدُكَ وَرَسُوْلُكَ.

‹26› O Allah, I seek protection in Your pleasure from Your anger, and in Your forgiveness from Your punishment. I seek protection from You through You. I cannot enumerate Your praise. You are as You have praised Yourself. (Abū Dāwūd)

‹27› O Allah, Lord of the kingdom, You grant kingdom to whoever you will, and You take kingdom away from whoever You will. You honour whoever You will and You disgrace whoever You will. All good is in Your hands. You are All-Powerful over everything. (O) the All-Merciful and the Very Merciful in this world and the hereafter; You give from them (this world and the hereafter) whomsoever You will and You withhold from them whomsoever You will. Have mercy on me which will leave me free of the mercy of those other than You. (Ṭabarānī)

«٢٦» اَللّٰهُمَّ إِنِّي أَعُوذُ بِرِضَاكَ مِنْ سَخَطِكَ ، وَبِمُعَافَاتِكَ مِنْ عُقُوبَتِكَ ، وَأَعُوذُ بِكَ مِنْكَ ، لَا أُحْصِي ثَنَاءً عَلَيْكَ ، أَنْتَ كَمَا أَثْنَيْتَ عَلَى نَفْسِكَ.

«٢٧» اَللّٰهُمَّ مَالِكَ الْمُلْكِ ، تُؤْتِي الْمُلْكَ مَنْ تَشَاءُ ، وَتَنْزِعُ الْمُلْكَ مِمَّنْ تَشَاءُ ، وَتُعِزُّ مَنْ تَشَاءُ ، وَتُذِلُّ مَنْ تَشَاءُ ، بِيَدِكَ الْخَيْرُ ، إِنَّكَ عَلَى كُلِّ شَيْءٍ قَدِيرٌ. رَحْمَنَ الدُّنْيَا وَالْآخِرَةِ وَرَحِيمَهُمَا ، تُعْطِيهِمَا مَنْ تَشَاءُ ، وَتَمْنَعُ مِنْهُمَا مَنْ تَشَاءُ ، اِرْحَمْنِي رَحْمَةً تُغْنِينِي بِهَا عَنْ رَحْمَةِ مَنْ سِوَاكَ.

‹28› O Allah, I beg You as I bear witness that You are Allah, there is no god worthy of worship except You, the One, the Self-Sufficient Master, who has not given birth and was not born, and to whom none is equal. (Tirmidhī)

‹29› O Allah, I beg You as all praise only belongs to You. There is no god worthy of worship except You, the Giver of all good, the Originator of the heavens and the earth. O Lord of Majesty and Honour, O the Ever Living, O the One who sustains and protects all that exists. (Abū Dāwūd)

‹30› O Allah, honour and have mercy upon Muḥammad and the family of Muḥammad as You have honoured and had mercy upon Ibrāhīm and the family of Ibrāhīm. Indeed, You are the Most Praiseworthy, the Most Glorious. O Allah, bless Muḥammad and the family of Muḥammad as You have blessed Ibrāhīm and the family of Ibrāhīm. Indeed, You are the Most Praiseworthy, the Most Glorious. (Bukhārī)

‹۲۸› اَللّٰهُمَّ إِنِّي أَسْأَلُكَ بِأَنِّي أَشْهَدُ أَنَّكَ أَنْتَ اللهُ لَا
إِلٰهَ إِلَّا أَنْتَ الْأَحَدُ الصَّمَدُ ، الَّذِي لَمْ يَلِدْ ، وَلَمْ
يُولَدْ ، وَلَمْ يَكُنْ لَّهُ كُفُوًا أَحَدٌ.

‹۲۹› اَللّٰهُمَّ إِنِّي أَسْأَلُكَ بِأَنَّ لَكَ الْحَمْدَ ، لَا إِلٰهَ إِلَّا
أَنْتَ الْمَنَّانُ ، بَدِيعُ السَّمٰوَاتِ وَالْأَرْضِ ، يَا ذَا
الْجَلَالِ وَالْإِكْرَامِ ، يَا حَيُّ يَا قَيُّومُ.

‹۳۰› اَللّٰهُمَّ صَلِّ عَلَى مُحَمَّدٍ وَعَلَى آلِ مُحَمَّدٍ ، كَمَا
صَلَّيْتَ عَلَى إِبْرَاهِيمَ وَعَلَى آلِ إِبْرَاهِيمَ ، إِنَّكَ
حَمِيدٌ مَجِيدٌ ، اَللّٰهُمَّ بَارِكْ عَلَى مُحَمَّدٍ وَعَلَى آلِ
مُحَمَّدٍ ، كَمَا بَارَكْتَ عَلَى إِبْرَاهِيمَ وَعَلَى آلِ
إِبْرَاهِيمَ ، إِنَّكَ حَمِيدٌ مَجِيدٌ.

❨31❩ O Allah, honour and have mercy upon Muḥammad and his household, as You have honoured and had mercy upon the family of Ibrāhīm. Indeed, You are the Most Praiseworthy, the Most Glorious. O Allah, honour and have mercy upon us alongside them. O Allah, bless Muḥammad and his household as You have blessed the family of Ibrāhīm. Indeed You are the Most Praiseworthy, the Most Glorious. O Allah, bless us alongside them. May the blessings of Allah and the prayers of the believers be for Muḥammad, the unlettered Prophet. (Dāraquṭnī)

❨32❩ O Allah, honour and have mercy upon Muḥammad, his spouses and his progeny as You have honoured and had mercy on the family of Ibrāhīm. Bless Muḥammad, his spouses and his progeny as You have blessed the family of Ibrāhīm. Indeed, You are the Most Praiseworthy, the Most Glorious. (Bukhārī)

(٣١) اَللّٰهُمَّ صَلِّ عَلَىٰ مُحَمَّدٍ وَعَلَىٰ آلِ بَيْتِهِ ، كَمَا صَلَّيْتَ عَلَىٰ آلِ إِبْرَاهِيمَ ، إِنَّكَ حَمِيدٌ مَجِيدٌ ، اَللّٰهُمَّ صَلِّ عَلَيْنَا مَعَهُمْ ، اَللّٰهُمَّ بَارِكْ عَلَىٰ مُحَمَّدٍ وَعَلَىٰ آلِ بَيْتِهِ ، كَمَا بَارَكْتَ عَلَىٰ آلِ إِبْرَاهِيمَ ، إِنَّكَ حَمِيدٌ مَجِيدٌ ، اَللّٰهُمَّ بَارِكْ عَلَيْنَا مَعَهُمْ ، صَلَوَاتُ اللهِ وَصَلَاةُ الْمُؤْمِنِينَ عَلَىٰ مُحَمَّدٍ النَّبِيِّ الْأُمِّيِّ.

(٣٢) اَللّٰهُمَّ صَلِّ عَلَىٰ مُحَمَّدٍ وَأَزْوَاجِهِ وَذُرِّيَّتِهِ ، كَمَا صَلَّيْتَ عَلَىٰ آلِ إِبْرَاهِيمَ ، وَبَارِكْ عَلَىٰ مُحَمَّدٍ وَأَزْوَاجِهِ وَذُرِّيَّتِهِ ، كَمَا بَارَكْتَ عَلَىٰ آلِ إِبْرَاهِيمَ ، إِنَّكَ حَمِيدٌ مَجِيدٌ.

ADDITIONAL
ḤAMD & ṢALAWĀT

الأدعية القرآنية

DU'ĀS FROM
THE QUR'ĀN

‹1› In the name of Allah, the All-Merciful, the Very Merciful. All praises and thanks are for Allah, the Lord of all the worlds, the All-Merciful, the Very Merciful, Master of the Day of Judgement. You Alone we worship, You Alone we ask for help. Guide us on the Straight Path, the path of those whom You have favoured, not of those who incur (Your) anger nor of those who have gone astray. (1:1-7)

‹2› There is no god worthy of worship except You. You are free from imperfection. Indeed, I have been of the wrongdoers. (21:87)

‹3› My Lord, I have certainly wronged myself, so forgive me. (28:16)

‹4› Our Lord, we have wronged ourselves. If You do not forgive us and have mercy upon us, we will surely be amongst the losers. (7:23)

‹5› You are our Protector, so forgive us and have mercy upon us. You are the best of those who forgive. (7:155)

﴿١١﴾ بِسْمِ اللَّهِ الرَّحْمٰنِ الرَّحِيمِ. اَلْحَمْدُ لِلَّهِ رَبِّ الْعٰلَمِينَ. الرَّحْمٰنِ الرَّحِيمِ. مٰلِكِ يَوْمِ الدِّينِ. إِيَّاكَ نَعْبُدُ وَإِيَّاكَ نَسْتَعِينُ. اِهْدِنَا الصِّرَاطَ الْمُسْتَقِيمَ. صِرَاطَ الَّذِينَ أَنْعَمْتَ عَلَيْهِمْ غَيْرِ الْمَغْضُوبِ عَلَيْهِمْ وَلَا الضَّآلِّينَ.

﴿٢١﴾ لَا إِلٰهَ إِلَّا أَنْتَ سُبْحٰنَكَ إِنِّي كُنْتُ مِنَ الظّٰلِمِينَ.

﴿٣١﴾ رَبِّ إِنِّي ظَلَمْتُ نَفْسِي فَاغْفِرْ لِي.

﴿٤١﴾ رَبَّنَا ظَلَمْنَا أَنْفُسَنَا وَإِنْ لَمْ تَغْفِرْ لَنَا وَتَرْحَمْنَا لَنَكُونَنَّ مِنَ الْخٰسِرِينَ.

﴿٥١﴾ أَنْتَ وَلِيُّنَا فَاغْفِرْ لَنَا وَارْحَمْنَا وَأَنْتَ خَيْرُ الْغٰفِرِينَ.

‹6› Our Lord, indeed we have believed, so forgive us our sins and protect us from the punishment of the Fire. (3:16)

‹7› Our Lord, we have believed, so forgive us and have mercy upon us: You are the Best of those who are merciful. (23:109)

‹8› My Lord, forgive and have mercy. You are the Best of those who are merciful. (23:118)

‹9› My Lord, I seek Your protection from asking You anything about which I have no knowledge. And unless You forgive me and have mercy upon me, I shall be amongst the losers. (11:47)

‹10› Our Lord, forgive us and our brothers who preceded us in faith. Do not put in our hearts any hatred toward those who have believed. Our Lord, indeed You are the Most Compassionate, the Ever-Merciful. (59:10)

‹11› Our Lord, perfect for us our light and forgive us. Indeed, You are All-Powerful over everything. (66:08)

﴿٦﴾ رَبَّنَا إِنَّنَا آمَنَّا فَاغْفِرْ لَنَا ذُنُوبَنَا وَقِنَا عَذَابَ النَّارِ.

﴿٧﴾ رَبَّنَا آمَنَّا فَاغْفِرْ لَنَا وَارْحَمْنَا وَأَنْتَ خَيْرُ الرَّاحِمِينَ.

﴿٨﴾ رَبِّ اغْفِرْ وَارْحَمْ وَأَنْتَ خَيْرُ الرَّاحِمِينَ.

﴿٩﴾ رَبِّ إِنِّي أَعُوذُ بِكَ أَنْ أَسْأَلَكَ مَا لَيْسَ لِي بِهِ عِلْمٌ، وَإِلَّا تَغْفِرْ لِي وَتَرْحَمْنِي أَكُنْ مِنَ الْخَاسِرِينَ.

﴿١٠﴾ رَبَّنَا اغْفِرْ لَنَا وَلِإِخْوَانِنَا الَّذِينَ سَبَقُونَا بِالْإِيْمَنِ، وَلَا تَجْعَلْ فِي قُلُوبِنَا غِلًّا لِلَّذِينَ ءَامَنُوا رَبَّنَا إِنَّكَ رَءُوفٌ رَحِيمٌ.

﴿١١﴾ رَبَّنَا أَتْمِمْ لَنَا نُورَنَا وَاغْفِرْ لَنَا إِنَّكَ عَلَىٰ كُلِّ شَيْءٍ قَدِيرٌ.

‹12› My Lord, build for me, near You, a house in Paradise. (66:11)

‹13› Our Lord, turn away from us the punishment of Hell-fire. Indeed, its punishment is endless. Indeed it is an evil residence and abode. (25:65-6)

‹14› Our Lord, You have not created all this (the heavens and the earth) without purpose- You are free from any defects- so protect us from the torment of the Fire. Our Lord, indeed whoever You admit to the Fire, You have disgraced him, and for the wrongdoers there are no helpers. Our Lord, indeed we have heard a caller calling to faith, [saying], ‹Believe in your Lord,› so we have believed. Our Lord, forgive us our sins, wipe out our bad deeds, and let us die with the truly righteous. Our Lord, bestow upon us all that You have promised us through Your messengers and do not humiliate us on the Day of Resurrection. Indeed, You never break Your promise. (3:191-4)

‹15› Our Lord, You have encompassed all things in mercy and knowledge, so forgive those who have repented and followed Your path, and protect them from the punishment of Hell-fire.

‹۱۲› رَبِّ ابْنِ لِي عِنْدَكَ بَيْتًا فِي الْجَنَّةِ.

‹۱۳› رَبَّنَا اصْرِفْ عَنَّا عَذَابَ جَهَنَّمَ ، إِنَّ عَذَابَهَا كَانَ غَرَامًا. إِنَّهَا سَآءَتْ مُسْتَقَرًّا وَّمُقَامًا.

‹۱۵› رَبَّنَا مَا خَلَقْتَ هَذَا بَطِلًا ، سُبْحَنَكَ فَقِنَا عَذَابَ النَّارِ. رَبَّنَا إِنَّكَ مَنْ تُدْخِلِ النَّارَ فَقَدْ أَخْزَيْتَهُ ، وَمَا لِلظَّلِمِينَ مِنْ أَنْصَارٍ. رَبَّنَا إِنَّنَا سَمِعْنَا مُنَادِيًا يُّنَادِي لِلْإِيمَنِ أَنْ آمِنُوا بِرَبِّكُمْ فَآمَنَّا، رَبَّنَا فَاغْفِرْ لَنَا ذُنُوبَنَا وَكَفِّرْ عَنَّا سَيِّئَاتِنَا وَتَوَفَّنَا مَعَ الْأَبْرَارِ. رَبَّنَا وَآتِنَا مَا وَعَدتَّنَا عَلَى رُسُلِكَ وَلَا تُخْزِنَا يَوْمَ الْقِيَمَةِ ، إِنَّكَ لَا تُخْلِفُ الْمِيعَادَ.

‹۱۵› رَبَّنَا وَسِعْتَ كُلَّ شَيْءٍ رَّحْمَةً وَّعِلْمًا، فَاغْفِرْ لِلَّذِينَ تَابُوا وَاتَّبَعُوا سَبِيلَكَ وَقِهِمْ عَذَابَ الْجَحِيمِ.

Our Lord, admit them to the eternal gardens of Paradise which You have promised them, along with whoever was righteous from their fathers, their spouses and their children. Indeed, You, and only You, are the All-Mighty and All-Wise. Protect them from all evil deeds. You will have bestowed Your mercy on those You protect from the evil deeds on that Day: that is the greatest achievement indeed. (40:7-9)

❨16❩ My Lord, truly I am in dire need of any good which You may send me. (28:24)

❨17❩ Our Lord, grant us good in this world and good in the Hereafter, and protect us from the torment of the Fire. (2:201)

❨18❩ Our Lord, grant us from Yourself mercy and provide us with guidance in our matter. (18:10)

❨19❩ Our Lord, do not let our hearts swerve from the truth after You have guided us, and bestow upon us mercy from Yourself. Surely, You, and You Alone, are the Great Bestower. (3:8)

❨20❩ My Lord, increase me in knowledge. (20:114)

رَبَّنَا وَأَدْخِلْهُمْ جَنَّاتِ عَدْنٍ الَّتِي وَعَدْتَّهُمْ وَمَنْ صَلَحَ مِنْ آبَائِهِمْ وَأَزْوَاجِهِمْ وَذُرِّيَّاتِهِمْ ، إِنَّكَ أَنتَ الْعَزِيزُ الْحَكِيمُ. وَقِهِمُ السَّيِّئَاتِ ، وَمَن تَقِ السَّيِّئَاتِ يَوْمَئِذٍ فَقَدْ رَحِمْتَهُ ، وَذَٰلِكَ هُوَ الْفَوْزُ الْعَظِيمُ.

‹١٦› رَبِّ إِنِّي لِمَا أَنزَلْتَ إِلَيَّ مِنْ خَيْرٍ فَقِيرٌ.

‹١٧› رَبَّنَا آتِنَا فِي الدُّنْيَا حَسَنَةً وَفِي الْآخِرَةِ حَسَنَةً وَقِنَا عَذَابَ النَّارِ.

‹١٨› رَبَّنَا آتِنَا مِن لَّدُنكَ رَحْمَةً وَهَيِّئْ لَنَا مِنْ أَمْرِنَا رَشَدًا.

‹١٩› رَبَّنَا لَا تُزِغْ قُلُوبَنَا بَعْدَ إِذْ هَدَيْتَنَا وَهَبْ لَنَا مِن لَّدُنكَ رَحْمَةً إِنَّكَ أَنتَ الْوَهَّابُ.

‹٢٠› رَبِّ زِدْنِي عِلْمًا.

‹21› My Lord, put my heart at peace for me, and make my task easy for me. (20:25)

‹22› My Lord, grant me wisdom and join me with the righteous. And grant that I may be spoken of with honour amongst the later generations. And make me amongst those who will inherit the Garden of Bliss... And do not disgrace me on the Day they will be resurrected - the Day when neither wealth nor children will be of any use - except for the one who comes to Allah with a sound heart. (26:83-89)

‹23› My Lord, make me steadfast in ṣalāh, and my offspring as well. Our Lord, accept my prayer. Our Lord, forgive me, my parents, and all the believers on the Day when the Reckoning will take place. (14:40-1)

‹24› My Lord, have mercy upon them (my parents) as they raised and nurtured me when I was young. (17:24)

‹25› My Lord, grant me from Yourself pious offspring. Indeed, You hear all prayers. (3:38)

‹٢١› رَبِّ اشْرَحْ لِي صَدْرِي. وَيَسِّرْ لِي أَمْرِي.

‹٢٢› رَبِّ هَبْ لِي حُكْمًا وَأَلْحِقْنِي بِالصَّالِحِينَ.
وَاجْعَلْ لِي لِسَانَ صِدْقٍ فِي الْآخِرِينَ.
وَاجْعَلْنِي مِنْ وَرَثَةِ جَنَّةِ النَّعِيمِ... وَلَا تُخْزِنِي
يَوْمَ يُبْعَثُونَ. يَوْمَ لَا يَنْفَعُ مَالٌ وَلَا بَنُونَ.
إِلَّا مَنْ أَتَى اللهَ بِقَلْبٍ سَلِيمٍ.

‹٢٣› رَبِّ اجْعَلْنِي مُقِيمَ الصَّلَاةِ وَمِنْ ذُرِّيَّتِي رَبَّنَا
وَتَقَبَّلْ دُعَاءِ. رَبَّنَا اغْفِرْ لِي وَلِوَالِدَيَّ وَلِلْمُؤْمِنِينَ
يَوْمَ يَقُومُ الْحِسَابُ.

‹٢٤› رَبِّ ارْحَمْهُمَا كَمَا رَبَّيَانِي صَغِيرًا.

‹٢٥› رَبِّ هَبْ لِي مِنْ لَدُنْكَ ذُرِّيَّةً طَيِّبَةً ، إِنَّكَ سَمِيعُ
الدُّعَاءِ.

‹26› My Lord, grant me (offspring) from amongst the righteous. (37:100)

‹27› My Lord, do not leave me childless, though You are the best of inheritors. (21:89)

‹28› Our Lord, grant us spouses and offspring who will be a joy to our eyes, and make us leaders of those who have taqwā (piety). (25:74)

‹29› My Lord, enable me to be grateful for Your favour which You have bestowed upon me and upon my parents, and to do good deeds that please You. And admit me by Your mercy amongst Your righteous servants. (27:19)

Make my offspring righteous; I truly repent to you, and truly I am of those who submit to You. (46:15)

‹30› My Lord, I seek protection with You from the promptings of the devils; and I seek protection in You, my Lord, from their coming near me. (23:97)

﴿٢٦﴾ رَبِّ هَبْ لِي مِنَ الصَّلِحِينَ.

﴿٢٧﴾ رَبِّ لَا تَذَرْنِي فَرْدًا وَّأَنْتَ خَيْرُ الْوَرِثِينَ.

﴿٢٨﴾ رَبَّنَا هَبْ لَنَا مِنْ أَزْوَجِنَا وَذُرِّيَّتِنَا قُرَّةَ أَعْيُنٍ وَّاجْعَلْنَا لِلْمُتَّقِينَ إِمَامًا.

﴿٢٩﴾ رَبِّ أَوْزِعْنِي أَنْ أَشْكُرَ نِعْمَتَكَ الَّتِي أَنْعَمْتَ عَلَيَّ وَعَلَى وَالِدَيَّ وَأَنْ أَعْمَلَ صَالِحًا تَرْضٰهُ، وَأَدْخِلْنِي بِرَحْمَتِكَ فِي عِبَادِكَ الصَّلِحِينَ.
وَأَصْلِحْ لِي فِي ذُرِّيَّتِي، إِنِّي تُبْتُ إِلَيْكَ وَإِنِّي مِنَ الْمُسْلِمِينَ.

﴿٣٠﴾ رَبِّ أَعُوذُ بِكَ مِنْ هَمَزَتِ الشَّيَطِينِ. وَأَعُوذُ بِكَ رَبِّ أَنْ يَّحْضُرُونِ.

‹31› Our Lord, do not impose blame upon us if we have forgotten or erred. Our Lord, and do not lay upon us a burden as You laid upon those before us. Our Lord, and do not burden us with that which we have no ability to bear. Pardon us, forgive us and have mercy upon us. You are our Protector, so help us against the disbelieving people. (2:285-6)

‹32› Our Lord, forgive us our sins and our extravagance in our affairs. Make our feet firm, and help us against the disbelieving people. (3:147)

‹33› Our Lord, pour upon us patience, make our steps firm and grant us victory over the disbelieving people. (2:250)

‹34› My Lord, support me against the people who spread corruption. (29:30)

‹35› Our Lord, do not let us join the wrongdoing people. (7:47)

﴾٣١﴿ رَبَّنَا لَا تُؤَاخِذْنَا إِنْ نَسِينَا أَوْ أَخْطَأْنَا ، رَبَّنَا وَلَا تَحْمِلْ عَلَيْنَا إِصْرًا كَمَا حَمَلْتَهُ عَلَى الَّذِينَ مِنْ قَبْلِنَا ، رَبَّنَا وَلَا تُحَمِّلْنَا مَا لَا طَاقَةَ لَنَا بِهِ ، وَاعْفُ عَنَّا وَاغْفِرْ لَنَا وَارْحَمْنَا أَنْتَ مَوْلَانَا فَانْصُرْنَا عَلَى الْقَوْمِ الْكَافِرِينَ.

﴾٣٢﴿ رَبَّنَا اغْفِرْ لَنَا ذُنُوبَنَا وَإِسْرَافَنَا فِي أَمْرِنَا وَثَبِّتْ أَقْدَامَنَا وَانْصُرْنَا عَلَى الْقَوْمِ الْكَافِرِينَ.

﴾٣٣﴿ رَبَّنَا أَفْرِغْ عَلَيْنَا صَبْرًا وَثَبِّتْ أَقْدَامَنَا وَانْصُرْنَا عَلَى الْقَوْمِ الْكَافِرِينَ.

﴾٣٤﴿ رَبِّ انْصُرْنِي عَلَى الْقَوْمِ الْمُفْسِدِينَ.

﴾٣٥﴿ رَبَّنَا لَا تَجْعَلْنَا مَعَ الْقَوْمِ الظَّالِمِينَ.

‹36› Our Lord, do not make us victims of the oppressors. Save us, through Your mercy, from the disbelieving people. (10:85-6)

‹37› Our Lord, in You Alone we trust, and to You Alone we turn, and to You is the ultimate return. Our Lord, do not let us be persecuted by those who disbelieve, and forgive us, our Lord. Indeed You, and only You, are the All-Mighty, the All-Wise. (60:4-5)

‹38› (My Lord), indeed adversity has touched me, and you are the Most Merciful of the merciful. (21:83)

‹39› (O Allah), Originator of the heavens and the earth, You are my Protector in this world and in the Hereafter. Make me die a Muslim and join me with the righteous. (12:101)

‹40› Our Lord, accept from us. Indeed, You - and You alone - are the All-Hearing, the All-Knowing. And accept our repentance. Indeed, You - and You Alone - are the Acceptor of repentance, the Very Merciful. (2:127-8)

﴿٣٦﴾ رَبَّنَا لَا تَجْعَلْنَا فِتْنَةً لِّلْقَوْمِ الظَّالِمِينَ. وَنَجِّنَا بِرَحْمَتِكَ مِنَ الْقَوْمِ الْكَافِرِينَ.

﴿٣٧﴾ رَبَّنَا عَلَيْكَ تَوَكَّلْنَا وَإِلَيْكَ أَنَبْنَا وَإِلَيْكَ الْمَصِيرُ. رَبَّنَا لَا تَجْعَلْنَا فِتْنَةً لِّلَّذِينَ كَفَرُوا وَاغْفِرْ لَنَا رَبَّنَا إِنَّكَ أَنتَ الْعَزِيزُ الْحَكِيمُ.

﴿٣٨﴾ (رَبِّ) أَنِّي مَسَّنِيَ الضُّرُّ وَأَنتَ أَرْحَمُ الرَّاحِمِينَ.

﴿٣٩﴾ (اللّٰهُمَّ يَا) فَاطِرَ السَّمٰوٰتِ وَالْأَرْضِ أَنتَ وَلِيِّي فِي الدُّنْيَا وَالْآخِرَةِ تَوَفَّنِي مُسْلِمًا وَأَلْحِقْنِي بِالصَّالِحِينَ.

﴿٤٠﴾ رَبَّنَا تَقَبَّلْ مِنَّا إِنَّكَ أَنتَ السَّمِيعُ الْعَلِيمُ. وَتُبْ عَلَيْنَا إِنَّكَ أَنتَ التَّوَّابُ الرَّحِيمُ.

"And your Lord said:
'Call upon Me;
I will respond to you.'"
(40:60)

الأدعية النبوية

DU'ĀS FROM
THE SUNNAH

‹1› (**Sayyid al-Istighfār**) O Allah, You are my Lord. There is no god worthy of worship except You. You have created me, and I am Your slave. I am under Your covenant and pledge (to fulfil it) to the best of my ability. I seek Your protection from the evil that I have done. I acknowledge the favours that You have bestowed upon me, and I admit my sins. Forgive me, for none forgives sins but You. (Bukhārī)

‹2› O Allah, You are the King, there is no god worthy of worship except You. You are my Lord and I am Your slave. I have wronged myself and I confess my sins. Forgive all of my sins; indeed no one forgives sins except You. Guide me to the best of character, for no one guides to the best of it except You; and turn the evil of it away from me, for no one turns it away except You. Here I am at Your service, seeking Your pleasure; all good is in Your hands and no evil is attributed to You. I am from You and I am returning to You. You are Most Blessed and You are Most Exalted. I seek Your forgiveness and repent to You. (Muslim)

«۱۱» (سَيِّدُ الاسْتِغْفَار) اَللَّهُمَّ أَنْتَ رَبِّي لَا إِلَهَ إِلَّا أَنْتَ، خَلَقْتَنِي وَأَنَا عَبْدُكَ، وَأَنَا عَلَى عَهْدِكَ وَوَعْدِكَ مَا اسْتَطَعْتُ، أَعُوذُ بِكَ مِنْ شَرِّ مَا صَنَعْتُ، أَبُوءُ لَكَ بِنِعْمَتِكَ عَلَيَّ وَأَبُوءُ لَكَ بِذَنْبِي، فَاغْفِرْ لِي فَإِنَّهُ لَا يَغْفِرُ الذُّنُوبَ إِلَّا أَنْتَ.

«۱۲» اَللَّهُمَّ أَنْتَ الْمَلِكُ لَا إِلَهَ إِلَّا أَنْتَ، أَنْتَ رَبِّي وَأَنَا عَبْدُكَ، ظَلَمْتُ نَفْسِي وَاعْتَرَفْتُ بِذَنْبِي، فَاغْفِرْ لِي ذُنُوبِي جَمِيعًا، إِنَّهُ لَا يَغْفِرُ الذُّنُوبَ إِلَّا أَنْتَ، وَاهْدِنِي لِأَحْسَنِ الْأَخْلَاقِ لَا يَهْدِي لِأَحْسَنِهَا إِلَّا أَنْتَ، وَاصْرِفْ عَنِّي سَيِّئَهَا لَا يَصْرِفُ عَنِّي سَيِّئَهَا إِلَّا أَنْتَ، لَبَّيْكَ وَسَعْدَيْكَ، وَالْخَيْرُ كُلُّهُ فِي يَدَيْكَ، وَالشَّرُّ لَيْسَ إِلَيْكَ، أَنَا بِكَ وَإِلَيْكَ، تَبَارَكْتَ وَتَعَالَيْتَ، أَسْتَغْفِرُكَ وَأَتُوبُ إِلَيْكَ.

‹3› O Allah, forgive my mistakes, ignorance, transgression in my matters, and what You are more Knowledgeable of than me. O Allah, forgive me for what I did in earnestness and in jest; unintentionally or intentionally; as I have committed all of these (types of sins). O Allah, forgive me for what I have already done, what I am yet to do, what I did publicly, what I did privately, and what You are more Knowledgeable of than me. You are the One who brings forward and You are the One who defers. You are All-Powerful over everything. (Muslim)

‹4› O Allah, You are the Ever-Pardoning; You love to pardon so pardon me. (Tirmidhī)

‹5› O Allah, Lord of Muḥammad, forgive my sins, remove the anger of my heart and protect me from misleading trials. (Ibn al-Sunnī)

‹6› O Allah, forgive for me all of my sins: the minor and major, the first and the last, the public and the private. (Muslim)

‹٣› اَللّٰهُمَّ اغْفِرْ لِي خَطِيئَتِي وَجَهْلِي وَإِسْرَافِي فِي أَمْرِي ، وَمَا أَنْتَ أَعْلَمُ بِهِ مِنِّي ، اَللّٰهُمَّ اغْفِرْ لِي جِدِّي وَهَزْلِي وَخَطَئِي وَعَمْدِي وَكُلُّ ذٰلِكَ عِنْدِي ، اَللّٰهُمَّ اغْفِرْ لِي مَا قَدَّمْتُ وَمَا أَخَّرْتُ ، وَمَا أَسْرَرْتُ وَمَا أَعْلَنْتُ ، وَمَا أَنْتَ أَعْلَمُ بِهِ مِنِّي ، أَنْتَ الْمُقَدِّمُ وَأَنْتَ الْمُؤَخِّرُ ، وَأَنْتَ عَلَى كُلِّ شَيْءٍ قَدِيرٌ.

‹٤› اَللّٰهُمَّ إِنَّكَ عَفُوٌّ تُحِبُّ الْعَفْوَ فَاعْفُ عَنِّي.

‹٥› اَللّٰهُمَّ رَبَّ مُحَمَّدٍ، اغْفِرْ لِي ذَنْبِي، وَأَذْهِبْ غَيْظَ قَلْبِي، وَأَعِذْنِي مِنْ مُضِلَّاتِ الْفِتَنِ.

‹٦› اَللّٰهُمَّ اغْفِرْ لِي ذَنْبِي كُلَّهُ ، دِقَّهُ وَجِلَّهُ ، وَأَوَّلَهُ وَآخِرَهُ ، وَعَلَانِيَتَهُ وَسِرَّهُ.

‹7› O Allah, I have wronged myself greatly and no one forgives sins except You; so grant me forgiveness from You and have mercy upon me. You are the Most Forgiving, the Most Merciful. (Bukhārī)

‹8› O Allah, forgive me, have mercy on me, grant me wellbeing, guide me and grant me sustenance. (Abū Dāwūd)

‹9› O Allah, distance me from my sins as You have distanced the East from the West. O Allah, purify me from my sins as white cloth is purified from dirt. O Allah, wash away my sins with snow, water and hail. (Muslim)

‹10› O Allah, forgive the believing men and the believing women. (Ṭabarānī)

«٧» اَللّٰهُمَّ إِنِّي ظَلَمْتُ نَفْسِي ظُلْمًا كَثِيرًا ، وَلَا يَغْفِرُ الذُّنُوبَ إِلَّا أَنْتَ ، فَاغْفِرْ لِي مَغْفِرَةً مِّنْ عِنْدِكَ ، وَارْحَمْنِي ، إِنَّكَ أَنْتَ الْغَفُورُ الرَّحِيمُ.

«٨» اَللّٰهُمَّ اغْفِرْ لِي ، وَارْحَمْنِي ، وَعَافِنِي ، وَاهْدِنِي وَارْزُقْنِي.

«٩» اَللّٰهُمَّ بَاعِدْ بَيْنِي وَبَيْنَ خَطَايَايَ كَمَا بَاعَدْتَ بَيْنَ الْمَشْرِقِ وَالْمَغْرِبِ ، اَللّٰهُمَّ نَقِّنِي مِنْ خَطَايَايَ كَمَا يُنَقَّى الثَّوْبُ الْأَبْيَضُ مِنَ الدَّنَسِ ، اَللّٰهُمَّ اغْسِلْنِي مِنْ خَطَايَايَ بِالثَّلْجِ وَالْمَاءِ وَالْبَرَدِ.

«١٠» اَللّٰهُمَّ اغْفِرْ لِلْمُؤْمِنِينَ وَالْمُؤْمِنَاتِ.

‹11› O Allah, I beg you for faith which does not waver, blessings which do not cease, and the company of our Prophet Muḥammad ﷺ in the loftiest abode of the Eternal Garden. (Ibn Ḥibbān)

‹12› O Allah, I beg you for al-Firdaws, the loftiest abode of Paradise. (Tirmidhī)

‹13› O Allah, Lord of Jibrā'īl and Mīkā'īl, and the Lord of Isrāfīl, I seek Your protection from the heat of the Hell-fire and from the punishment of the grave. (Nasā'ī)

‹14› O Allah, I seek Your protection from the punishment of the Hell-fire, and from the punishment of the grave, and from the trials of life and death, and from the evil of the tribulation of Dajjāl, the false Messiah. (Muslim)

‹15› O Allah, I seek Your protection from the anguish of the world and the anguish of the Day of Judgement. (Abū Dāwūd)

«١١» اَللّٰهُمَّ إِنِّي أَسْأَلُكَ إِيمَانًا لَّا يَرْتَدُّ ، وَنَعِيمًا لَّا يَنْفَدُ ، وَمُرَافَقَةَ نَبِيِّنَا مُحَمَّدٍ فِي أَعْلَى جَنَّةِ الْخُلْدِ.

«١٢» اَللّٰهُمَّ إِنِّي أَسْأَلُكَ الْفِرْدَوْسَ أَعْلَى الْجَنَّةِ.

«١٣» اَللّٰهُمَّ رَبَّ جَبْرَائِيلَ وَمِيكَائِيلَ وَرَبَّ إِسْرَافِيلَ ، أَعُوذُ بِكَ مِنْ حَرِّ النَّارِ ، وَمِنْ عَذَابِ الْقَبْرِ.

«١٤» اَللّٰهُمَّ إِنِّي أَعُوذُ بِكَ مِنْ عَذَابِ جَهَنَّمَ ، وَمِنْ عَذَابِ الْقَبْرِ ، وَمِنْ فِتْنَةِ الْمَحْيَا وَالْمَمَاتِ ، وَمِنْ شَرِّ فِتْنَةِ الْمَسِيحِ الدَّجَّالِ.

«١٥» اَللّٰهُمَّ إِنِّي أَعُوذُ بِكَ مِنْ ضِيقِ الدُّنْيَا وَضِيقِ يَوْمِ الْقِيَامَةِ.

‹16› O Allah, we beg You for all that which will necessitate Your mercy and the determination to do all that which will necessitate Your forgiveness; for protection from every sin and accomplishment of every good; for attainment of Paradise and for freedom from Hell-fire. (Ḥākim)

‹17› O Allah, grant me an easy reckoning. (Aḥmad)

‹18› O Allah, grant us Your blessings, Your mercy, Your grace and Your sustenance in abundance. O Allah, I beg you for eternal blessings which do not change nor disappear. O Allah, I beg you for blessings on the day of intense need and safety on the day of fear (i.e. Day of Judgement). O Allah, I seek Your protection from the evil of what You have granted us and the evil of what You have withheld from us. O Allah, endear faith to us and beautify it in our hearts. Make disbelief, sins and disobedience hateful to us, and make us of the rightly guided ones. O Allah, grant us death as Muslims, make us live as Muslims and join us with the righteous without being humiliated or tested. O Allah, fight the disbelievers who reject Your Messengers and avert from Your path. Inflict

«١٦» اَللّٰهُمَّ إِنَّا نَسْأَلُكَ مُوجِبَاتِ رَحْمَتِكَ ، وَعَزَائِمَ مَغْفِرَتِكَ، وَالسَّلَامَةَ مِنْ كُلِّ إِثْمٍ، وَالْغَنِيمَةَ مِنْ كُلِّ بِرٍّ، وَالْفَوْزَ بِالْجَنَّةِ، وَالنَّجَاةَ مِنَ النَّارِ.

«١٧» اَللّٰهُمَّ حَاسِبْنِي حِسَابًا يَسِيرًا.

«١٨» اَللّٰهُمَّ ابْسُطْ عَلَيْنَا مِنْ بَرَكَاتِكَ وَرَحْمَتِكَ وَفَضْلِكَ وَرِزْقِكَ ، اَللّٰهُمَّ إِنِّي أَسْأَلُكَ النَّعِيمَ الْمُقِيمَ الَّذِي لَا يَحُولُ وَلَا يَزُولُ، اَللّٰهُمَّ إِنِّي أَسْأَلُكَ النَّعِيمَ يَوْمَ الْعَيْلَةِ، وَالْأَمْنَ يَوْمَ الْخَوْفِ، اَللّٰهُمَّ إِنِّي عَائِذٌ بِكَ مِنْ شَرِّ مَا أَعْطَيْتَنَا وَشَرِّ مَا مَنَعْتَنَا، اَللّٰهُمَّ حَبِّبْ إِلَيْنَا الْإِيمَانَ وَزَيِّنْهُ فِي قُلُوبِنَا ، وَكَرِّهْ إِلَيْنَا الْكُفْرَ وَالْفُسُوقَ وَالْعِصْيَانَ ، وَاجْعَلْنَا مِنَ الرَّاشِدِينَ، اَللّٰهُمَّ تَوَفَّنَا مُسْلِمِينَ ، وَأَحْيِنَا مُسْلِمِينَ ، وَأَلْحِقْنَا

upon them Your punishment and vengeance. O Allah, fight the disbelievers who were given the Book, O the True God. (Aḥmad)

‹19› O Allah, grant me the best of what You grant Your righteous slaves. (Ibn Ḥibbān)

‹20› O Allah, I beg you for martyrdom in Your path. (Muslim)

‹21› O Allah, I beg you for a pure life, a good death, and a return (to You) which is neither humiliating nor disgraceful. (Ṭabarānī)

‹22› O the Ever-Living, the One who sustains and protects all that exists; I seek assistance through Your mercy. Rectify all of my affairs and do not entrust me to myself for the blink of an eye. (Nasā'ī)

‹23› O Allah, keep faith rejuvenated in my heart. (Ḥākim)

بِالصَّالِحِينَ ، غَيْرَ خَزَايَا وَلَا مَفْتُونِينَ ، اَللّٰهُمَّ قَاتِلِ الْكَفَرَةَ الَّذِينَ يُكَذِّبُونَ رُسُلَكَ ، وَيَصُدُّونَ عَنْ سَبِيلِكَ ، وَاجْعَلْ عَلَيْهِمْ رِجْزَكَ وَعَذَابَكَ ، اَللّٰهُمَّ قَاتِلِ الْكَفَرَةَ الَّذِينَ أُوتُوا الْكِتَابَ ، إِلٰهَ الْحَقِّ.

«۱۹» اَللّٰهُمَّ آتِنِيْ أَفْضَلَ مَا تُؤْتِيْ عِبَادَكَ الصَّالِحِينَ.

«۲۰» اَللّٰهُمَّ إِنِّيْ أَسْأَلُكَ شَهَادَةً فِيْ سَبِيلِكَ.

«۲۱» اَللّٰهُمَّ إِنِّيْ أَسْأَلُكَ عِيْشَةً نَقِيَّةً ، وَمِيْتَةً سَوِيَّةً ، وَمَرَدًّا غَيْرَ مُخْزٍ وَّلَا فَاضِح.

«۲۲» يَا حَيُّ يَا قَيُّوْمُ ، بِرَحْمَتِكَ أَسْتَغِيْثُ ، أَصْلِحْ لِيْ شَأْنِيْ كُلَّهُ ، وَلَا تَكِلْنِيْ إِلَى نَفْسِيْ طَرْفَةَ عَيْنٍ.

«۲۳» اَللّٰهُمَّ جَدِّدِ الْإِيْمَانَ فِيْ قَلْبِيْ.

‹24› O Allah, safeguard me with Islam whilst I am standing. Safeguard me with Islam whilst I am sitting. Safeguard me with Islam whilst I am sleeping, and do not let an enemy or envier gloat over my misery. O Allah, I beg You for all good, the treasures of which are in Your Hand. I seek Your protection from all evil, the treasures of which are in Your Hand. (Ḥākim)

‹25› O Allah, Turner of hearts, make my heart firm upon Your religion. (Tirmidhī)

‹26› O Allah, Changer of hearts, direct our hearts to Your obedience. (Muslim)

‹27› O Guardian of Islam and its followers, keep me firm on it (Islam) until I meet You. (Ṭabarānī)

‹28› O Allah, grant us the best outcome in all of our affairs, and protect us from the humiliation of this world and the punishment of the hereafter. (Aḥmad)

«٢٤» اَللّٰهُمَّ احْفَظْنِي بِالْإِسْلَامِ قَائِمًا ، وَاحْفَظْنِي بِالْإِسْلَامِ قَاعِدًا ، وَاحْفَظْنِي بِالْإِسْلَامِ رَاقِدًا ، وَلَا تُشْمِتْ بِي عَدُوًّا وَلَا حَاسِدًا ، اَللّٰهُمَّ إِنِّي أَسْأَلُكَ مِنْ كُلِّ خَيْرٍ خَزَائِنُهُ بِيَدِكَ ، وَأَعُوذُ بِكَ مِنْ كُلِّ شَرٍّ خَزَائِنُهُ بِيَدِكَ.

«٢٥» يَا مُقَلِّبَ الْقُلُوبِ ثَبِّتْ قَلْبِي عَلَى دِينِكَ.

«٢٦» اَللّٰهُمَّ مُصَرِّفَ الْقُلُوبِ صَرِّفْ قُلُوبَنَا عَلَى طَاعَتِكَ.

«٢٧» يَا وَلِيَّ الْإِسْلَامِ وَأَهْلِهِ ، ثَبِّتْنِي بِهِ حَتَّى أَلْقَاكَ.

«٢٨» اَللّٰهُمَّ أَحْسِنْ عَاقِبَتَنَا فِي الْأُمُورِ كُلِّهَا ، وَأَجِرْنَا مِنْ خِزْيِ الدُّنْيَا وَعَذَابِ الْآخِرَةِ.

‹29› O Allah, I beg you for steadfastness in all matters and the determination to take the right course. I ask You for all that which will necessitate Your mercy and the determination to do all that which will necessitate Your forgiveness. I ask You to make me grateful for Your blessings and to worship You in an excellent manner. I ask You for a sound heart and a truthful tongue. I ask You for the good of what You know, I seek Your protection from the evil of what You know, and I seek Your forgiveness for what You know. Indeed, You are the All-Knowing of the unseen. (Aḥmad)

‹30› O Allah, I ask You for well-being in this world and the next. O Allah, I ask You for forgiveness and well-being in my religion, in my worldly affairs, in my family and in my wealth. O Allah, conceal my faults and calm my fears. O Allah, guard me from in front of me and behind me, from my right, and from my left, and from above me. I seek protection in Your greatness from being unexpectedly destroyed from beneath me. (Abū Dāwūd)

﴿٢٩﴾ اَللّٰهُمَّ إِنِّي أَسْأَلُكَ الثَّبَاتَ فِي الْأَمْرِ، وَالْعَزِيمَةَ عَلَى الرُّشْدِ، وَأَسْأَلُكَ مُوجِبَاتِ رَحْمَتِكَ، وَعَزَائِمَ مَغْفِرَتِكَ، وَأَسْأَلُكَ شُكْرَ نِعْمَتِكَ، وَحُسْنَ عِبَادَتِكَ، وَأَسْأَلُكَ قَلْبًا سَلِيمًا، وَلِسَانًا صَادِقًا، وَأَسْأَلُكَ مِنْ خَيْرِ مَا تَعْلَمُ، وَأَعُوذُ بِكَ مِنْ شَرِّ مَا تَعْلَمُ، وَأَسْتَغْفِرُكَ لِمَا تَعْلَمُ، إِنَّكَ أَنْتَ عَلَّامُ الْغُيُوبِ.

﴿٣٠﴾ اَللّٰهُمَّ إِنِّي أَسْأَلُكَ الْعَافِيَةَ فِي الدُّنْيَا وَالْآخِرَةِ، اَللّٰهُمَّ إِنِّي أَسْأَلُكَ الْعَفْوَ وَالْعَافِيَةَ فِي دِينِي وَدُنْيَايَ وَأَهْلِي وَمَالِي، اَللّٰهُمَّ اسْتُرْ عَوْرَاتِي وَآمِنْ رَوْعَاتِي، اَللّٰهُمَّ احْفَظْنِي مِنْ بَيْنِ يَدَيَّ، وَمِنْ خَلْفِي، وَعَنْ يَمِينِي، وَعَنْ شِمَالِي، وَمِنْ فَوْقِي، وَأَعُوذُ بِعَظَمَتِكَ أَنْ أُغْتَالَ مِنْ تَحْتِي.

‹31› My Lord, help me and do not help others against me. Grant me victory and do not grant victory to others over me. Plan in my favour and do not plan for others against me. Guide me and ease guidance for me. Help me against those who oppress me. My Lord, make me one who is extremely grateful to You, who remembers you always, who perpetually fears You, who is fully obedient to You, who is humble before You, who constantly cries and pleads with You, and who repeatedly turns to You in repentance. My Lord, accept my repentance, wash away my sins, accept my supplications, strengthen my case, rectify my speech, guide my heart, and remove the malice from my heart. (Tirmidhī)

‹32› O Allah, help me in remembering You, in being grateful to You, and in worshipping You in an excellent manner. (Abū Dāwūd)

‹33› O Allah, I beg You to enable me to do good deeds, abstain from evil acts, and love the poor; and that You forgive me and have mercy upon me. When You intend to test a people, then grant me death without being tested. I ask You for Your love, the love of those whom You love, and the love of deeds which will bring me closer to Your love. (Tirmidhī)

﴿۳۱﴾ رَبِّ أَعِنِّي وَلَا تُعِنْ عَلَيَّ ، وَانْصُرْنِي وَلَا تَنْصُرْ عَلَيَّ ، وَامْكُرْ لِي وَلَا تَمْكُرْ عَلَيَّ ، وَاهْدِنِي وَيَسِّرِ الْهُدَى لِي ، وَانْصُرْنِي عَلَى مَنْ بَغَى عَلَيَّ ، رَبِّ اجْعَلْنِي لَكَ شَكَّارًا ، لَكَ ذَكَّارًا ، لَكَ رَهَّابًا ، لَكَ مِطْوَاعًا ، لَكَ مُخْبِتًا ، إِلَيْكَ أَوَّاهًا مُنِيبًا ، رَبِّ تَقَبَّلْ تَوْبَتِي ، وَاغْسِلْ حَوْبَتِي ، وَأَجِبْ دَعْوَتِي ، وَثَبِّتْ حُجَّتِي ، وَسَدِّدْ لِسَانِي ، وَاهْدِ قَلْبِي ، وَاسْلُلْ سَخِيمَةَ صَدْرِي.

﴿۳۲﴾ اَللَّهُمَّ أَعِنِّي عَلَى ذِكْرِكَ وَشُكْرِكَ وَحُسْنِ عِبَادَتِكَ.

﴿۳۳﴾ اَللَّهُمَّ إِنِّي أَسْأَلُكَ فِعْلَ الْخَيْرَاتِ ، وَتَرْكَ الْمُنْكَرَاتِ ، وَحُبَّ الْمَسَاكِينِ ، وَأَنْ تَغْفِرَ لِي وَتَرْحَمَنِي ، وَإِذَا أَرَدْتَ فِتْنَةَ قَوْمٍ فَتَوَفَّنِي غَيْرَ مَفْتُونٍ ، وَأَسْأَلُكَ حُبَّكَ ، وَحُبَّ مَنْ يُحِبُّكَ ، وَحُبَّ عَمَلٍ يُقَرِّبُنِي إِلَى حُبِّكَ.

⟨34⟩ O Allah, grant me Your love and the love of those whose love will benefit me with You. O Allah, whatever You have provided me of the things that I love, make them a source of strength for me in pursuing what You love. O Allah, whatever you have withheld from me from what I love, make its absence a means for me to pursue what You love. (Tirmidhī)

⟨35⟩ O Allah, with Your knowledge of the unseen and Your absolute power over the creation, let me live in this world as long as You know my living is good for me; and give me death when You know death is better for me. O Allah, I ask You for Your fear in private and in public, and for the word of truth in times of joy and anger. I ask You for moderation in wealth and in poverty. I ask You for endless blessings and perpetual delights. I ask You to make me pleased with destiny; for a cool and comfortable life after death; for the pleasure of seeing Your Face; and for the longing to meet You, without any painful ordeals and tribulations that misguide. O Allah, adorn us with the beauty of faith, and make us those who guide others and are guided themselves. (Nasā'ī)

«٣٤» اَللّٰهُمَّ ارْزُقْنِي حُبَّكَ ، وَحُبَّ مَنْ يَنْفَعُنِي حُبُّهُ عِنْدَكَ ، اَللّٰهُمَّ مَا رَزَقْتَنِي مِمَّا أُحِبُّ فَاجْعَلْهُ قُوَّةً لِّي فِيمَا تُحِبُّ ، اَللّٰهُمَّ مَا زَوَيْتَ عَنِّي مِمَّا أُحِبُّ فَاجْعَلْهُ فَرَاغًا لِّي فِيمَا تُحِبُّ.

«٣٥» اَللّٰهُمَّ بِعِلْمِكَ الْغَيْبَ ، وَقُدْرَتِكَ عَلَى الْخَلْقِ ، أَحْيِنِي مَا عَلِمْتَ الْحَيَاةَ خَيْرًا لِّي ، وَتَوَفَّنِي إِذَا عَلِمْتَ الْوَفَاةَ خَيْرًا لِّي ، اَللّٰهُمَّ إِنِّي أَسْأَلُكَ خَشْيَتَكَ فِي الْغَيْبِ وَالشَّهَادَةِ ، وَأَسْأَلُكَ كَلِمَةَ الْحَقِّ فِي الرِّضَا وَالْغَضَبِ ، وَأَسْأَلُكَ الْقَصْدَ فِي الْغِنَى وَالْفَقْرِ ، وَأَسْأَلُكَ نَعِيمًا لَّا يَنْفَدُ ، وَأَسْأَلُكَ قُرَّةَ عَيْنٍ لَّا تَنْقَطِعُ ، وَأَسْأَلُكَ الرِّضَا بَعْدَ الْقَضَاءِ ، وَأَسْأَلُكَ بَرْدَ الْعَيْشِ بَعْدَ الْمَوْتِ ، وَأَسْأَلُكَ لَذَّةَ النَّظَرِ إِلَى وَجْهِكَ ، وَالشَّوْقَ إِلَى لِقَائِكَ ، فِي غَيْرِ ضَرَّاءَ مُضِرَّةٍ ، وَلَا فِتْنَةٍ مُّضِلَّةٍ ، اَللّٰهُمَّ زَيِّنَّا بِزِينَةِ الْإِيمَانِ ، وَاجْعَلْنَا هُدَاةً مُّهْتَدِينَ.

‹36› O Allah, I beg You for all good: the immediate and the delayed, what I know of and what I do not know. I seek Your protection from all evil: the immediate and the delayed, what I know of and what I do not know. O Allah, I beg You for the good which Your slave and Prophet ﷺ asked from You, and I seek Your protection from the evil which Your slave and Prophet ﷺ sought protection for from You. O Allah, I beg You for Paradise, and whatever words or actions lead to it. I seek Your protection from Hell-fire, and whatever words or actions lead to it. I ask You to decree good for me in everything You foreordain for me. (Aḥmad)

‹37› O Allah, I beg You for the best of what can be asked for, the best supplication, the ultimate success, the best deeds, the best reward, the best life, and the best death. Keep me steadfast, make my scales heavy, establish my belief, elevate my ranks, accept my ṣalāh, forgive my sins and I ask You for lofty ranks in Paradise. O Allah, I beg you for good beginnings, good endings, good in its entirety, its

اَللّٰهُمَّ إِنِّي أَسْأَلُكَ مِنَ الْخَيْرِ كُلِّهِ عَاجِلِهِ وَآجِلِهِ ،
مَا عَلِمْتُ مِنْهُ وَمَا لَمْ أَعْلَمْ ، وَأَعُوذُ بِكَ مِنَ
الشَّرِّ كُلِّهِ عَاجِلِهِ وَآجِلِهِ ، مَا عَلِمْتُ مِنْهُ وَمَا
لَمْ أَعْلَمْ ، اَللّٰهُمَّ إِنِّي أَسْأَلُكَ مِنْ خَيْرِ مَا سَأَلَكَ
عَبْدُكَ وَنَبِيُّكَ ، وَأَعُوذُ بِكَ مِنْ شَرِّ مَا عَاذَ
مِنْهُ عَبْدُكَ وَنَبِيُّكَ ، اَللّٰهُمَّ إِنِّي أَسْأَلُكَ الْجَنَّةَ ،
وَمَا قَرَّبَ إِلَيْهَا مِنْ قَوْلٍ أَوْ عَمَلٍ ، وَأَعُوذُ بِكَ
مِنَ النَّارِ ، وَمَا قَرَّبَ إِلَيْهَا مِنْ قَوْلٍ أَوْ عَمَلٍ ،
وَأَسْأَلُكَ أَنْ تَجْعَلَ كُلَّ قَضَاءٍ قَضَيْتَهُ لِي خَيْرًا.

«۳۷» اَللّٰهُمَّ إِنِّي أَسْأَلُكَ خَيْرَ الْمَسْأَلَةِ ، وَخَيْرَ الدُّعَاءِ ،
وَخَيْرَ النَّجَاحِ ، وَخَيْرَ الْعَمَلِ ، وَخَيْرَ الثَّوَابِ ،
وَخَيْرَ الْحَيَاةِ ، وَخَيْرَ الْمَمَاتِ ، وَثَبِّتْنِي ، وَثَقِّلْ
مَوَازِينِي ، وَحَقِّقْ إِيمَانِي ، وَارْفَعْ دَرَجَاتِي ،
وَتَقَبَّلْ صَلَاتِي ، وَاغْفِرْ خَطِيئَتِي ، وَأَسْأَلُكَ

first, its apparent and its hidden; and lofty ranks in Paradise. Āmīn. O Allah, I beg you for the best of what I can do, perform and accomplish, the best of what is hidden or apparent; and lofty ranks in Paradise. Āmīn. O Allah, I beg you to elevate my mention, remove my burden, rectify my affairs, purify my heart, protect my chastity, enlighten my heart, forgive my sins and I ask You for lofty ranks in Paradise. Āmīn. O Allah, I beg you to bless for me my inner self, my hearing, my sight, my soul, my appearance, my character, my family, my life, my death and my deeds. Accept my good deeds and I ask You for lofty ranks in Paradise. Āmīn. (Ḥākim)

The definition of Āmīn (آمِيْن) is: 'O Allah, accept my duʿāʾ.'

ᴥᴥᴥᴥᴥᴥᴥᴥᴥᴥ

Āmīn is the seal of the Lord of the worlds, it is with it that His servants seal their duʿāʾ.'

ʿAlī ibn Abī Ṭālib ☙

الدَّرَجَاتِ الْعُلَا مِنَ الْجَنَّةِ ، اَللَّهُمَّ إِنِّي أَسْأَلُكَ
فَوَاتِحَ الْخَيْرِ ، وَخَوَاتِمَهُ ، وَجَوَامِعَهُ ، وَأَوَّلَهُ ،
وَظَاهِرَهُ ، وَبَاطِنَهُ ، وَالدَّرَجَاتِ الْعُلَا مِنَ الْجَنَّةِ
آمِين ، اَللَّهُمَّ إِنِّي أَسْأَلُكَ خَيْرَ مَا آتِي ، وَخَيْرَ مَا
أَفْعَلُ ، وَخَيْرَ مَا أَعْمَلُ ، وَخَيْرَ مَا بَطَنَ ، وَخَيْرَ مَا
ظَهَرَ ، وَالدَّرَجَاتِ الْعُلَا مِنَ الْجَنَّةِ آمِين ، اَللَّهُمَّ
إِنِّي أَسْأَلُكَ أَنْ تَرْفَعَ ذِكْرِي ، وَتَضَعَ وِزْرِي ،
وَتُصْلِحَ أَمْرِي ، وَتُطَهِّرَ قَلْبِي ، وَتُحَصِّنَ فَرْجِي ،
وَتُنَوِّرَ لِي قَلْبِي ، وَتَغْفِرَ لِي ذَنْبِي ، وَأَسْأَلُكَ
الدَّرَجَاتِ الْعُلَا مِنَ الْجَنَّةِ آمِين ، اَللَّهُمَّ إِنِّي
أَسْأَلُكَ أَنْ تُبَارِكَ لِي فِي نَفْسِي ، وَفِي سَمْعِي ، وَفِي
بَصَرِي ، وَفِي رُوحِي ، وَفِي خَلْقِي ، وَفِي خُلُقِي ،
وَفِي أَهْلِي ، وَفِي مَحْيَايَ ، وَفِي مَمَاتِي ، وَفِي عَمَلِي ،
فَتَقَبَّلْ حَسَنَاتِي ، وَأَسْأَلُكَ الدَّرَجَاتِ الْعُلَا مِنَ
الْجَنَّةِ ، آمِين.

‹38› O Allah, place light in my heart, light in my tongue, light in my hearing and light in my sight. Place light above me, light beneath me, light on my right, light on my left, light in front of me, and light behind me. Place light in my self and magnify for me light. (Muslim)

‹39› O Allah, I am Your slave and the son of Your male slave and the son of Your female slave. My forehead is in Your Hand (i.e. you have control over me). I am subject to Your judgement and Your decree concerning me is just. I ask You - by every name that is Yours, by which You have named Yourself, or taught any one of Your creation, or revealed in Your Book, or kept unto Yourself in the knowledge of the unseen that is with You - to make the Qur'ān the spring of my heart, the light of my chest, the banisher of my grief and the reliever of my anxiety. (Aḥmad)

٣٨» اَللّٰهُمَّ اجْعَلْ لِّيْ فِيْ قَلْبِيْ نُوْرًا ، وَفِيْ لِسَانِيْ نُوْرًا ، وَفِيْ سَمْعِيْ نُوْرًا ، وَفِيْ بَصَرِيْ نُوْرًا ، وَمِنْ فَوْقِيْ نُوْرًا ، وَمِنْ تَحْتِيْ نُوْرًا ، وَعَنْ يَّمِيْنِيْ نُوْرًا ، وَعَنْ شِمَالِيْ نُوْرًا ، وَمِنْ بَيْنِ يَدَيَّ نُوْرًا ، وَمِنْ خَلْفِيْ نُوْرًا ، وَاجْعَلْ فِيْ نَفْسِيْ نُوْرًا ، وَأَعْظِمْ لِيْ نُوْرًا.

٣٩» اَللّٰهُمَّ إِنِّيْ عَبْدُكَ ، وَابْنُ عَبْدِكَ ، وَابْنُ أَمَتِكَ ، نَاصِيَتِيْ بِيَدِكَ ، مَاضٍ فِيَّ حُكْمُكَ ، عَدْلٌ فِيَّ قَضَاؤُكَ ، أَسْأَلُكَ بِكُلِّ اسْمٍ هُوَ لَكَ ، سَمَّيْتَ بِهِ نَفْسَكَ ، أَوْ عَلَّمْتَهُ أَحَدًا مِّنْ خَلْقِكَ ، أَوْ أَنْزَلْتَهُ فِيْ كِتَابِكَ ، أَوِ اسْتَأْثَرْتَ بِهِ فِيْ عِلْمِ الْغَيْبِ عِنْدَكَ ، أَنْ تَجْعَلَ الْقُرْآنَ رَبِيْعَ قَلْبِيْ ، وَنُوْرَ صَدْرِيْ ، وَجَلَاءَ حُزْنِيْ ، وَذَهَابَ هَمِّيْ.

‹40› O Allah, rectify my religion for me which is the protection of my affairs. Rectify my world for me wherein is my livelihood. Rectify my hereafter for me, to which is my return. Make my life a means of increase for me in every good, and make death a respite for me from every evil. (Muslim)

‹41› O Allah, apportion for us enough fear and awe of You to prevent us from sinning against You, and enough obedience to You to make us reach Your Paradise, and enough certainty to make the difficulties of this world easy for us. O Allah, let us enjoy our hearing and sight and strength as long as You allow us to live, and make it an inheritance for us. Let our retaliation be upon those who have wronged us, and help us against those who harbour enmity towards us. Let not our afflictions be in our religion. Do not make the world our biggest concern or the full extent of our knowledge, and do not give power over us to anyone who will not have mercy on us. (Tirmidhī)

«٤٠» اَللّٰهُمَّ أَصْلِحْ لِيْ دِيْنِيَ الَّذِيْ هُوَ عِصْمَةُ أَمْرِيْ ، وَأَصْلِحْ لِيْ دُنْيَايَ الَّتِيْ فِيْهَا مَعَاشِيْ ، وَأَصْلِحْ لِيْ آخِرَتِيَ الَّتِيْ فِيْهَا مَعَادِيْ ، وَاجْعَلِ الْحَيَاةَ زِيَادَةً لِّيْ فِيْ كُلِّ خَيْرٍ ، وَاجْعَلِ الْمَوْتَ رَاحَةً لِّيْ مِنْ كُلِّ شَرٍّ.

«٤١» اَللّٰهُمَّ اقْسِمْ لَنَا مِنْ خَشْيَتِكَ مَا يَحُوْلُ بِهٖ بَيْنَنَا وَبَيْنَ مَعَاصِيْكَ ، وَمِنْ طَاعَتِكَ مَا تُبَلِّغُنَا بِهٖ جَنَّتَكَ ، وَمِنَ الْيَقِيْنِ مَا تُهَوِّنُ بِهٖ عَلَيْنَا مَصَائِبَ الدُّنْيَا ، اَللّٰهُمَّ مَتِّعْنَا بِأَسْمَاعِنَا ، وَأَبْصَارِنَا ، وَقُوَّتِنَا مَا أَحْيَيْتَنَا ، وَاجْعَلْهُ الْوَارِثَ مِنَّا ، وَاجْعَلْ ثَأْرَنَا عَلٰى مَنْ ظَلَمَنَا ، وَانْصُرْنَا عَلٰى مَنْ عَادَانَا ، وَلَا تَجْعَلْ مُصِيْبَتَنَا فِيْ دِيْنِنَا ، وَلَا تَجْعَلِ الدُّنْيَا أَكْبَرَ هَمِّنَا ، وَلَا مَبْلَغَ عِلْمِنَا ، وَلَا تُسَلِّطْ عَلَيْنَا مَنْ لَّا يَرْحَمُنَا.

‹42› O Allah, guide me amongst those You have guided, grant me wellbeing amongst those You have granted wellbeing, befriend me amongst those You have befriended. Bless me in what You have given me and protect me from the evil of what You have decreed. You are the One who decrees and You are not decreed against. Whomsoever You befriend will never be disgraced, and whomsoever You oppose will never be honoured. You are the Most Blessed, our Lord and You are the Most Exalted. (Abū Dāwūd)

‹43› O Allah, Lord of Jibrā'īl, Mīkā'īl and Isrāfīl, Creator of the heavens and the earth, Knower of the unseen and seen; You will judge between Your servants in what they used to differ. Guide me in what is contentious to the truth, by Your will. Indeed, You guide whomsoever You wish to a straight path. (Muslim)

«٤٢» اَللّٰهُمَّ اهْدِنِي فِيمَنْ هَدَيْتَ ، وَعَافِنِي فِيمَنْ عَافَيْتَ ، وَتَوَلَّنِي فِيمَنْ تَوَلَّيْتَ ، وَبَارِكْ لِي فِيمَا أَعْطَيْتَ ، وَقِنِي شَرَّ مَا قَضَيْتَ ، إِنَّكَ تَقْضِي وَلَا يُقْضَى عَلَيْكَ ، وَإِنَّهُ لَا يَذِلُّ مَنْ وَالَيْتَ ، وَلَا يَعِزُّ مَنْ عَادَيْتَ ، تَبَارَكْتَ رَبَّنَا وَتَعَالَيْتَ.

«٤٣» اَللّٰهُمَّ رَبَّ جَبْرَائِيلَ ، وَمِيكَائِيلَ ، وَإِسْرَافِيلَ ، فَاطِرَ السَّمٰوَاتِ وَالْأَرْضِ ، عَالِمَ الْغَيْبِ وَالشَّهَادَةِ ، أَنْتَ تَحْكُمُ بَيْنَ عِبَادِكَ فِيمَا كَانُوا فِيهِ يَخْتَلِفُونَ ، اهْدِنِي لِمَا اخْتُلِفَ فِيهِ مِنَ الْحَقِّ بِإِذْنِكَ ، إِنَّكَ تَهْدِي مَنْ تَشَاءُ إِلَى صِرَاطٍ مُّسْتَقِيمٍ.

‹44› O Allah, I beg You for guidance, taqwā (piety), chastity and self-sufficiency. (Muslim)

‹45› O Allah, guide me and grant me firmness. O Allah, I beg You for guidance and firmness (on the straight path). (Muslim)

‹46› O Allah, inspire me with sound guidance and protect me from the evil of my self. (Tirmidhī)

‹47› O Allah, to You Alone I submit, in You Alone I believe, upon You Alone I place my trust, to You Alone I turn repeatedly in repentance, and for You Alone I advocate. O Allah, I seek protection - with Your honour, there is no god worthy of worship except You - from misguidance. You are the Ever-Living who does not die, whereas the jinn and mankind die. (Muslim)

‹48› O Allah, grant me a deep understanding of the religion. (Bukhārī)

‹٤٤› اَللّٰهُمَّ إِنِّي أَسْأَلُكَ الْهُدَى وَالتُّقَى وَالْعَفَافَ وَالْغِنَى.

‹٤٥› اَللّٰهُمَّ اهْدِنِي وَسَدِّدْنِي، اَللّٰهُمَّ إِنِّي أَسْأَلُكَ الْهُدَى وَالسَّدَادَ.

‹٤٦› اَللّٰهُمَّ أَلْهِمْنِيْ رُشْدِيْ، وَأَعِذْنِيْ مِنْ شَرِّ نَفْسِيْ.

‹٤٧› اَللّٰهُمَّ لَكَ أَسْلَمْتُ، وَبِكَ آمَنْتُ، وَعَلَيْكَ تَوَكَّلْتُ، وَإِلَيْكَ أَنَبْتُ، وَبِكَ خَاصَمْتُ، اَللّٰهُمَّ إِنِّي أَعُوْذُ بِعِزَّتِكَ لَا إِلٰهَ إِلَّا أَنْتَ أَنْ تُضِلَّنِيْ، أَنْتَ الْحَيُّ الَّذِيْ لَا يَمُوْتُ، وَالْجِنُّ وَالْإِنْسُ يَمُوْتُوْنَ.

‹٤٨› اَللّٰهُمَّ فَقِّهْنِيْ فِي الدِّيْنِ.

‹49› O Allah, benefit me with what you have taught me, teach me what will benefit me, and increase me in knowledge. (Tirmidhī)

‹50› O Allah, I ask You for beneficial knowledge, wholesome sustenance, and deeds which are accepted. (Ibn Mājah)

‹51› O Allah, grant my soul taqwā (piety) and purify it, for You are the Best of those who can purify it. You are its Protector and Master. O Allah, I seek Your protection from knowledge which does not benefit, a heart which does not submit, a soul which is not satisfied and a supplication which is not accepted. (Muslim)

‹52› O Allah, I seek Your protection from knowledge which does not benefit, actions which are not raised (to You), a heart which does not humble itself (in Your awe), and an utterance which is not accepted. (Aḥmad)

‹53› O Allah, I seek Your protection from a prayer which does not benefit. (Abū Dāwūd)

«٤٩» اَللّٰهُمَّ انْفَعْنِي بِمَا عَلَّمْتَنِي، وَعَلِّمْنِي مَا يَنْفَعُنِي، وَزِدْنِي عِلْمًا.

«٥٠» اَللّٰهُمَّ إِنِّي أَسْأَلُكَ عِلْمًا نَافِعًا، وَرِزْقًا طَيِّبًا، وَعَمَلًا مُتَقَبَّلًا.

«٥١» اَللّٰهُمَّ آتِ نَفْسِي تَقْوَاهَا، وَزَكِّهَا أَنْتَ خَيْرُ مَنْ زَكَّاهَا، أَنْتَ وَلِيُّهَا وَمَوْلَاهَا، اَللّٰهُمَّ إِنِّي أَعُوذُ بِكَ مِنْ عِلْمٍ لَّا يَنْفَعُ، وَمِنْ قَلْبٍ لَّا يَخْشَعُ، وَمِنْ نَفْسٍ لَّا تَشْبَعُ، وَمِنْ دَعْوَةٍ لَّا يُسْتَجَابُ لَهَا.

«٥٢» اَللّٰهُمَّ إِنِّي أَعُوذُ بِكَ مِنْ عِلْمٍ لَّا يَنْفَعُ، وَعَمَلٍ لَّا يُرْفَعُ، وَقَلْبٍ لَّا يَخْشَعُ، وَقَوْلٍ لَّا يُسْمَعُ.

«٥٣» اَللّٰهُمَّ إِنِّي أَعُوذُ بِكَ مِنْ صَلَاةٍ لَّا تَنْفَعُ.

‹54› O Allah, I seek Your protection from knowingly associating partners with You and seek Your forgiveness for unknowingly (doing so). (Ibn al-Sunnī)

‹55› O Allah, I seek Your protection from miserliness and I seek Your protection from cowardice. I seek Your protection from being returned to the worst part of life (old age), I seek Your protection from the trials of the world, and I seek Your protection from the punishment of the grave. (Bukhārī)

‹56› O Allah, I seek Your protection from inability, laziness, cowardice, miserliness, senility, hard heartedness, heedlessness, economic dependence, humiliation and destitution. I seek Your protection from poverty, disbelief, disobedience, discord, hypocrisy, seeking fame and ostentation. I seek Your protection from deafness, dumbness, insanity, leprosy, vitiligo and from all harmful diseases. (Ḥākim)

﴿٥٤﴾ اَللَّهُمَّ إِنِّي أَعُوذُ بِكَ أَنْ أُشْرِكَ بِكَ وَأَنَا أَعْلَمُ ، وَأَسْتَغْفِرُكَ لِمَا لَا أَعْلَمُ.

﴿٥٥﴾ اَللَّهُمَّ إِنِّي أَعُوذُ بِكَ مِنَ الْبُخْلِ ، وَأَعُوذُ بِكَ مِنَ الْجُبْنِ ، وَأَعُوذُ بِكَ أَنْ أُرَدَّ إِلَى أَرْذَلِ الْعُمُرِ ، وَأَعُوذُ بِكَ مِنْ فِتْنَةِ الدُّنْيَا ، وَأَعُوذُ بِكَ مِنْ عَذَابِ الْقَبْرِ.

﴿٥٦﴾ اَللَّهُمَّ إِنِّي أَعُوذُ بِكَ مِنَ الْعَجْزِ ، وَالْكَسَلِ ، وَالْجُبْنِ ، وَالْبُخْلِ ، وَالْهَرَمِ ، وَالْقَسْوَةِ ، وَالْغَفْلَةِ ، وَالْعَيْلَةِ ، وَالذِّلَّةِ ، وَالْمَسْكَنَةِ ، وَأَعُوذُ بِكَ مِنَ الْفَقْرِ ، وَالْكُفْرِ ، وَالْفُسُوقِ ، وَالشِّقَاقِ ، وَالنِّفَاقِ ، وَالسُّمْعَةِ ، وَالرِّيَاءِ ، وَأَعُوذُ بِكَ مِنَ الصَّمَمِ ، وَالْبَكَمِ ، وَالْجُنُونِ ، وَالْجُذَامِ ، وَالْبَرَصِ ، وَسَيِّءِ الْأَسْقَامِ.

‹57› O Allah, I seek Your protection from senility, from death by falling from a height or being crushed to death; from dying of sorrow, being burnt or drowning to death. I seek Your protection from being struck by shayṭān at the time of death and that I am killed whilst I am fleeing from the battlefield. I seek Your protection from dying from a venomous sting. (Nasā'ī)

‹58› O Allah, I seek Your protection from the evil of what I have done, and from the evil of what I have not done. (Muslim)

‹59› O Allah, I seek Your protection from the evil of my hearing, the evil of my sight, the evil of my tongue, the evil of my heart and the evil of my semen. (Tirmidhī)

‹60› O Allah, I seek Your protection from evil character, evil actions and evil desires. (Tirmidhī)

‹۵۷› اَللّٰهُمَّ إِنِّي أَعُوذُ بِكَ مِنَ الْهَرَمِ ، وَالتَّرَدِّي ، وَالْهَدْمِ ، وَالْغَمِّ ، وَالْحَرِيقِ ، وَالْغَرَقِ ، وَأَعُوذُ بِكَ أَنْ يَتَخَبَّطَنِي الشَّيْطَانُ عِنْدَ الْمَوْتِ وَأَنْ أُقْتَلَ فِي سَبِيلِكَ مُدْبِرًا ، وَأَعُوذُ بِكَ أَنْ أَمُوتَ لَدِيغًا.

‹۵۸› اَللّٰهُمَّ إِنِّي أَعُوذُ بِكَ مِنْ شَرِّ مَا عَمِلْتُ ، وَمِنْ شَرِّ مَا لَمْ أَعْمَلْ.

‹۵۹› اَللّٰهُمَّ إِنِّي أَعُوذُ بِكَ مِنْ شَرِّ سَمْعِي ، وَمِنْ شَرِّ بَصَرِي ، وَمِنْ شَرِّ لِسَانِي ، وَمِنْ شَرِّ قَلْبِي ، وَمِنْ شَرِّ مَنِيِّي.

‹٦۰› اَللّٰهُمَّ إِنِّي أَعُوذُ بِكَ مِنْ مُنْكَرَاتِ الْأَخْلَاقِ ، وَالْأَعْمَالِ ، وَالْأَهْوَاءِ.

‹61› O Allah, I seek Your protection from the loss of Your favours, the removal of Your complete protection, Your sudden punishment and all that which may incur Your displeasure. (Muslim)

‹62› O Allah, I seek Your protection from hunger, as it is indeed an evil companion and I seek Your protection from treachery, as it is an evil confidante. (Nasā'ī)

‹63› O Allah, I seek Your protection from bad days, bad nights, bad moments, bad companions, and from bad neighbours in (permanent) places of residence. (Ṭabarānī)

‹64› O Allah, I seek Your protection from an evil neighbour; from a spouse who will age me ahead of time; from a child who will rule over me; from wealth that will become a punishment for me; from a cunning friend whose eyes see me yet his heart keeps guard over me: if he sees any good, he conceals it and if he sees any bad, he announces it. (Ṭabarānī)

﴿٦١﴾ اَللّٰهُمَّ إِنِّي أَعُوذُ بِكَ مِنْ زَوَالِ نِعْمَتِكَ، وَتَحَوُّلِ عَافِيَتِكَ، وَفُجَاءَةِ نِقْمَتِكَ، وَجَمِيعِ سَخَطِكَ.

﴿٦٢﴾ اَللّٰهُمَّ إِنِّي أَعُوذُ بِكَ مِنَ الْجُوعِ، فَإِنَّهُ بِئْسَ الضَّجِيعُ، وَأَعُوذُ بِكَ مِنَ الْخِيَانَةِ، فَإِنَّهَا بِئْسَتِ الْبِطَانَةُ.

﴿٦٣﴾ اَللّٰهُمَّ إِنِّي أَعُوذُ بِكَ مِنْ يَوْمِ السُّوءِ، وَمِنْ لَيْلَةِ السُّوءِ، وَمِنْ سَاعَةِ السُّوءِ، وَمِنْ صَاحِبِ السُّوءِ، وَمِنْ جَارِ السُّوءِ فِي دَارِ الْمُقَامَةِ.

﴿٦٤﴾ اَللّٰهُمَّ إِنِّي أَعُوذُ بِكَ مِنْ جَارِ السُّوءِ، وَمِنْ زَوْجٍ تُشَيِّبُنِي قَبْلَ الْمَشِيبِ، وَمِنْ وَلَدٍ يَكُونُ عَلَيَّ رَبًّا، وَمِنْ مَالٍ يَكُونُ عَلَيَّ عَذَابًا، وَمِنْ خَلِيلٍ مَاكِرٍ عَيْنُهُ تَرَانِي، وَقَلْبُهُ يَرْعَانِي، إِنْ رَأَى حَسَنَةً دَفَنَهَا، وَإِذَا رَأَى سَيِّئَةً أَذَاعَهَا.

‹65› O Allah, I seek Your protection from severe trials, wretchedness, bad fate and that my enemies rejoice in my misery. (Bukhārī)

‹66› O Allah, I seek Your protection from anxiety and grief. I seek Your protection from inability and laziness. I seek Your protection from cowardice and miserliness and I seek Your protection from being overcome by debt and being overpowered by men. (Abū Dāwūd)

‹67› O Allah, I seek Your protection from poverty, scarcity, humiliation; and I seek Your protection from oppressing or being oppressed. (Abū Dāwūd)

‹68› O Allah, suffice me with Your lawful against Your prohibited, and make me independent of all those besides You. (Tirmidhī)

«٦٥» اَللّٰهُمَّ إِنِّي أَعُوذُ بِكَ مِنْ جَهْدِ الْبَلَاءِ ، وَدَرَكِ الشَّقَاءِ ، وَسُوءِ الْقَضَاءِ ، وَشَمَاتَةِ الْأَعْدَاءِ.

«٦٦» اَللّٰهُمَّ إِنِّي أَعُوذُ بِكَ مِنَ الْهَمِّ وَالْحَزَنِ ، وَأَعُوذُ بِكَ مِنَ الْعَجْزِ وَالْكَسَلِ ، وَأَعُوذُ بِكَ مِنَ الْجُبْنِ وَالْبُخْلِ ، وَأَعُوذُ بِكَ مِنْ غَلَبَةِ الدَّيْنِ وَقَهْرِ الرِّجَالِ.

«٦٧» اَللّٰهُمَّ إِنِّي أَعُوذُ بِكَ مِنَ الْفَقْرِ ، وَالْقِلَّةِ ، وَالذِّلَّةِ ، وَأَعُوذُ بِكَ مِنْ أَنْ أَظْلِمَ أَوْ أُظْلَمَ.

«٦٨» اَللّٰهُمَّ اكْفِنِي بِحَلَالِكَ عَنْ حَرَامِكَ ، وَأَغْنِنِي بِفَضْلِكَ عَمَّنْ سِوَاكَ.

‹69› O Allah, make me content with what You have granted me, bless me in it and be a protector for me in that which is absent from me (i.e. family and wealth). (Ḥākim)

‹70› O Allah, forgive my sins, make my home spacious and bless me in what You have granted me. (Aḥmad)

‹71› O Allah, grant us more and not less. Honour us and do not disgrace us. Grant us and do not deprive us. Favour us and do not favour others over us. Make us pleased with You and be pleased with us. (Tirmidhī)

‹72› O Allah, beautify my character as You have beautified my appearance. (Aḥmad)

‹73› O Allah, any believing servant whom I have cursed, make that a source of nearness to You on the Day of Judgement. (Muslim)

«٦٩» اَللّٰهُمَّ قَنِّعْنِي بِمَا رَزَقْتَنِي ، وَبَارِكْ لِيْ فِيْهِ ، وَاخْلُفْ عَلَيَّ كُلَّ غَائِبَةٍ لِيْ بِخَيْرٍ.

«٧٠» اَللّٰهُمَّ اغْفِرْ لِي ذَنْبِيْ ، وَوَسِّعْ لِيْ فِيْ دَارِيْ ، وَبَارِكْ لِيْ فِيْمَا رَزَقْتَنِيْ.

«٧١» اَللّٰهُمَّ زِدْنَا وَلَا تَنْقُصْنَا ، وَأَكْرِمْنَا وَلَا تُهِنَّا ، وَأَعْطِنَا وَلَا تَحْرِمْنَا ، وَآثِرْنَا وَلَا تُؤْثِرْ عَلَيْنَا ، وَأَرْضِنَا وَارْضَ عَنَّا.

«٧٢» اَللّٰهُمَّ أَحْسَنْتَ خَلْقِيْ فَأَحْسِنْ خُلُقِيْ.

«٧٣» اَللّٰهُمَّ فَأَيُّمَا عَبْدٍ مُّؤْمِنٍ سَبَبْتُهُ فَاجْعَلْ ذٰلِكَ لَهُ قُرْبَةً إِلَيْكَ يَوْمَ الْقِيَامَةِ.

‹74› O Allah, unite our hearts, set aright our relationships, and guide us to the paths of peace. Bring us out of darknesses into light and protect us from evident and hidden obscenities. Bless us in our hearing, our sight, our hearts, our spouses and our children. Accept our repentance. Indeed, You truly are the Acceptor of repentance, the Ever-Merciful. Make us of those who are grateful for Your blessings, who praise You for them and acknowledge them. Perfect (the blessings) and make them last forever for us. (Ḥākim)

‹75› O Allah, we beg You for the good which Your Prophet Muḥammad ﷺ asked from You. We seek Your protection from the evil which Your Prophet Muḥammad ﷺ sought protection for from You. You are the One whose assistance is sought and You are the Only One who provides and suffices. There is no power (to avert evil) nor strength (to do good) except by Allah. (Tirmidhī)

‹٧٤› اَللّٰهُمَّ أَلِّفْ بَيْنَ قُلُوبِنَا ، وَأَصْلِحْ ذَاتَ بَيْنِنَا ،
وَاهْدِنَا سُبُلَ السَّلَامِ ، وَنَجِّنَا مِنَ الظُّلُمَاتِ
إِلَى النُّورِ ، وَجَنِّبْنَا الْفَوَاحِشَ مَا ظَهَرَ مِنْهَا
وَمَا بَطَنَ ، وَبَارِكْ لَنَا فِي أَسْمَاعِنَا ، وَأَبْصَارِنَا ،
وَقُلُوبِنَا ، وَأَزْوَاجِنَا ، وَذُرِّيَّاتِنَا ، وَتُبْ عَلَيْنَا
إِنَّكَ أَنْتَ التَّوَّابُ الرَّحِيمُ ، وَاجْعَلْنَا شَاكِرِينَ
لِنِعَمِكَ مُثْنِينَ بِهَا عَلَيْكَ ، قَابِلِينَ لَهَا ، وَأَتِمَّهَا
عَلَيْنَا.

‹٧٥› اَللّٰهُمَّ إِنَّا نَسْأَلُكَ مِنْ خَيْرِ مَا سَأَلَكَ مِنْهُ نَبِيُّكَ
مُحَمَّدٌ صَلَّى اللهُ عَلَيْهِ وَسَلَّمَ ، وَنَعُوذُ بِكَ مِنْ
شَرِّ مَا اسْتَعَاذَ مِنْهُ نَبِيُّكَ مُحَمَّدٌ صَلَّى اللهُ عَلَيْهِ
وَسَلَّمَ ، وَأَنْتَ الْمُسْتَعَانُ ، وَعَلَيْكَ الْبَلَاغُ ، وَلَا
حَوْلَ وَلَا قُوَّةَ إِلَّا بِاللهِ.

MY DU'Ā' LIST

Remember to be ambitious and ask Allah for everything.
Nothing is too big for the One being asked and nothing
is too small for the one asking Him.